WHY GREAT TEACHERS QUIT

To my parents, Anne and Don Farber.
And to my little daughters, Addy and Elly,
may you continue to grow, learn, love, and speak your mind.

WHY GREAT TEACHERS QUIT

AND HOW WE MIGHT STOP THE EXODUS

KATY FARBER

CORWIN
A SAGE Company

For information:

Corwin
A SAGE Company
2455 Teller Road
Thousand Oaks, California 91320
(800) 233-9936
Fax: (800) 417-2466
www.corwin.com

SAGE India Pvt. Ltd.
B 1/I 1 Mohan Cooperative
Industrial Area
Mathura Road,
New Delhi 110 044
India

SAGE Ltd.
1 Oliver's Yard
55 City Road
London EC1Y 1SP
United Kingdom

SAGE Asia-Pacific Pte. Ltd.
33 Pekin Street #02-01
Far East Square
Singapore 048763

Printed in the United States of America.

Library of Congress Cataloging-in-Publication Data

Farber, Katy.
Why great teachers quit : and how we might stop the exodus / Katy Farber ; foreword by Virginia Hines.
 p. cm.
Includes bibliographical references and index.
ISBN 978-1-4129-7245-1 (pbk.)
 1. Teacher turnover—United States—Prevention. 2. Teachers—Job stress—United States. 3. Employee retention—United States. 4. Burn out (Psychology)—Prevention. I. Title.

LB2833.2.F37 2010
371.14—dc22   2010014602

This book is printed on acid-free paper.

10   11   12   13   14   10   9   8   7   6   5   4   3   2   1

Acquisitions Editor:	Carol Chambers Collins
Associate Editor:	Megan Bedell
Editorial Assistant:	Sarah Bartlett
Production Editor:	Cassandra Margaret Seibel
Copy Editor:	Cynthia Long
Typesetter:	C&M Digitals (P) Ltd.
Proofreader:	Susan Schon
Indexer:	Jean Casalegno
Cover Designer:	Karine Hovsepian

Contents

Foreword   ix
by Virginia Hines

Preface   xiii

Acknowledgments   xix

About the Author   xxiii

"Guardian"   xxiv
by Katy Farber

Introduction   1

1. **Standardized Testing**   5
   Effects on School Climate   6
   Effects on Curriculum   6
   Effects on Teaching Schedules and
       Learning Outcomes   9
   Effects on Students   11
   Recommendations for Administrators
       and Teacher Leaders   14
   Words of Wisdom From Veteran Teachers   15
   The Silver Lining: Personally Fulfilling   16
   Hope on the Horizon: Reevaluating Our
       Standardized-Testing Culture   17
   Additional Resources   17

2. **Working Conditions in Today's Schools**   19
   Big Problem #1: Violence   20
   Big Problem #2: Unsafe Schools   22
   Small Problems That Add Up   27

Recommendations for Administrators
    and Teacher Leaders   28
Words of Wisdom From Veteran Teachers   33
Hope on the Horizon: Cities Adopt
    the Precautionary Principle   34
Success Stories: Green Schools   35
Additional Resources   37

3. Ever-Higher Expectations   43

Unrealistic Expectations   44
The Time Crunch: Do More With Less   44
Professional Development That Doesn't
    Speak to Real Concerns   46
The Threat to Health and Well-Being   47
Recommendations for Administrators and
    Teacher Leaders   50
Words of Wisdom From Veteran Teachers   52
Success Stories: Professional Learning
    Communities and Collaboration Time   53
The Silver Lining: Challenging and Always Changing   55
Additional Resources   57

4. Bureaucracy   59

Field Trips: No Good Deed Goes Unpunished   60
Committees: The Death of Creative Ideas   62
Purchase Orders and Closed Budgets   64
Scheduling: Not Ideal for Students or Teachers   65
Policy: Lack of Input   67
Recommendations for Administrators
    and Teacher Leaders   69
Words of Wisdom From Veteran Teachers   71
Success Stories: Real-Life Integrated Learning   72
The Silver Lining: Making a Difference   74
Additional Resources   75

5. Respect and Compensation   77

Struggling to Make Ends Meet   78
Paying for School Supplies   81
A Culture of Disrespect   83
The Martyr System: Do More for Free   86

Recommendations for Administrators
    and Teacher Leaders   88
Words of Wisdom From Veteran Teachers   89
Success Stories: A Decent Working Wage   90
Hope on the Horizon: Teacher Pay and Respect in
    New York and Other States   90
The Silver Lining: Helping Children Learn and Grow   94
Additional Resources   96

6. Parents   **97**

Unrealistic Demands and No Limits   99
My Child Is Always Right   101
Helicopter Parents: Micromanaging the Classroom   103
Recommendations for Administrators
    and Teacher Leaders   107
Words of Wisdom From Veteran Teachers   113
Success Stories: Partnering to Help a Child Read and
    Participate   116
The Silver Lining: Contributing to a
    Community Over Time   117
Additional Resources   118

7. Administrators   **121**

The Pressure Cooker of the Principalship   122
Pressure From Parents   123
Testing Pressure   124
Time Pressure   125
Mentors Help Principals, Too   129
Recommendations for Administrators
    and Teacher Leaders   130
Words of Wisdom From Veteran Teachers   133
Success Stories: Principal Mentors Make a Difference 134
Additional Resources   135

8. School Boards   **137**

Shared Leadership   138
Uses and Abuses of Power   140
Recommendations for Administrators
    and Teacher Leaders   142

Words of Wisdom From Veteran Teachers   145
Success Stories: School Board, Administrator,
    and Teacher Teams   146
The Silver Lining: Buoyed by a Supportive Community   148
Hope on the Horizon: Teaming Up With Teachers   150
Additional Resources   150

Afterword: Final Thoughts   **153**

References   **157**

Index   **163**

Foreword

E ach semester I ask the students in the course, Introduction to the Profession of Teaching (EDUC 101): "Why do you want to be a teacher?" Each semester the responses follow three general themes: I love children, I want to exemplify a teacher that influenced me, or I love my content area and I want others to love it too. While all of these rationales are noble, and I am sure genuine, they are not reasons that will sustain an educator through his or her teacher education program and through those first few years as a professional. It will take more than a love of children, a memory, or a passion of content to assure that a teacher will stay in the teaching profession for his or her career.

Nationwide, one of five teachers will leave the profession in their first year. That number grows to three in five during the first five years. There are numerous stories of why teachers leave; the job may not have been what the educator had idealized or the money may not be what was expected. A lack of motivated students, limited parental support, school violence, or the long hours of grading and planning that consume one's "life" may all be factors. Unfortunately, those factors that force teachers to abandon their chosen paths are growing.

At the end of five years, there are two teachers who stick it out: two teachers out of five have kept their commitment to themselves, their students, and the community. Who are they? What makes them stay? What makes them thrive in the gloom and doom of today's educational systems?

First and foremost, the teachers who have stayed in teaching are graduates from solid teacher education programs. They have worked hard in their academics and they have been active participants in their field experiences. They have developed skills of critical thinking, problem solving, and "with-it-ness." They are compassionate and caring. They understand human growth and development. They know their content and they possess the skills and knowledge needed for cognitive engineering. But these characteristics—even when tied to the love of children, fond memories of school, and a deep love of subject matter—will not be enough for a teacher to commit to the classroom for thirty years.

It takes more. It takes a keen understanding of who you are, what your role is in the scheme of things, and how your actions affect the actions of others. It takes a systems-thinking approach, efficacy, and reflection. Katy Farber, a former student of mine and the author of *Why Great Teachers Quit: And How We Might Stop the Exodus*, addresses some of the causes of teacher attrition. She writes compellingly about the various problems in schools that make it difficult for teachers to stay and teach. But one of the things that Katy does best in her book is to address the manners in which we can help teachers overcome those problems and thrive. She lists numerous suggestions and solutions to those varied factors and provides some great resources for teachers. A unique aspect of the text is Farber's ability to describe the nature of teaching within the concept of a larger system; educating children is not just the role of the educator, but the responsibility of all stakeholders in society. She presents the idea that we all have the power and the responsibility to assure the sustainability of the schoolhouse and the community. Educating learners is not a solitary task, but a system that provides opportunities for students, teachers, parents, and communities to grow. Educating learners also provides the means to sustain a global society, inspire innovation, and promote human dignity. If you as a teacher look closely at where your position is within that system and access the wide realm of resources available, then successful teaching will be your reward.

A YouTube sensation by the name of Sherman Dalton (Believe in Yourself, 2009) begins a speech to the Dallas ISD by stating, "I believe in me." He asks his audience, "Do you believe in me? Do you believe that I can stand up here fearless and talk to over twenty thousand of you?" Of course we believe in Dalton. We believe that he can reach his highest potential, that he will meet high expectations and make us proud. But that's not the part of his speech I want to focus on. Dalton asks the teachers and staff at that opening day meeting, "Do you believe in you?" Well do you? Do you believe that when you face your first class as a novice teacher that you can fearlessly make a difference in the lives of twenty-five learners? Do you believe that you can have a dramatic impact upon their motivation to learn? Do you believe that you can facilitate their respect of all individuals and facilitate their appreciation of differences among humankind? If you do believe in you, then you have efficacy. You have the knowledge that you can act as an agent of change. You are aware that what you do today will affect tomorrow in the lives of students, in the school-house, and in the greater society. You understand that you can improve the society we live in, help students meet their full potential, and be a powerful influence on making a better world.

Reflection is a term that is often given lip service in the teaching profession. Its application is limited; all too often it is overlooked for a packaged cure in teaching. What does reflection mean? How does it apply to an aspiring or seasoned teacher? Reflection is akin to responsibility. Responsibility is the ability to see oneself as cause, to take ownership of the decisions you make and the consequences of those decisions. John Dewey (1933) stated that the "active, persistent, and careful consideration of any belief or supposed form of knowledge in light of the grounds that support and the further conclusion to which it tends constitutes reflective thought" (pg. 9). In simpler terms, the educator needs to ask, "How do I know that? Is there evidence to support what I believe?" Real evidence, not something you have always heard or just looked up on Wikipedia. Evidence based in the context of classroom practice. Data: hard evidence that comes in the form of observations, assessment, and research. What Dewey wanted teachers to think about was "What is the impact of your actions upon your students? Do your perceptions and expectations affect students' achievement and behavior?" Numerous studies have enlightened us and made it clear that teachers' expectations have an effect upon student achievement. The lens that we use to view a learner will have an impact upon that student's engagement in class, their motivation to learn, and their perception of self. As Dalton states, "Here's the deal. I can do anything, be anything, create anything, dream anything, become anything. Because you believe in me. And it rubs off on me." The key here is that you think before you act. You are thoughtful about how you address a child or class. You analyze your students' needs and make plans accordingly. And you look yourself in the mirror and ask, "Are my students learning? Did I do the best job I could? How do I know this? What could I have done better?"

Teaching is a celebration of learning. It is a forum to affirm the importance of sustainability of culture and social justice. Teaching is an opportunity to set goals: for the future; for learners in classrooms, for stakeholders in communities, and even for our global village, Earth. In order to meet those goals, teachers will need more than a love of kids. Teachers will need to believe in the potential that each child brings to the classroom and make a concerted effort to help that child soar. In order to meet those goals, a teacher will need to draw upon the memories of those past great teachers, but also be a great teacher in her own right. He must be a teacher who is compassionate, caring, knowledgeable, and reflective. In order to meet those goals, a teacher will need to believe; to believe in students, parents, their communities, and greater society. Contemporary teachers must believe in the inherent good in every person and every opportunity. And most important, teachers must believe in their ability to make a change for the better. Do you believe in you?

Katy Farber believes in you, and in your ability to sustain good teaching and become an agent of change in your school.

Virginia Hines, EdD
Professor, School of Education
Ferris State University

Preface

I did not intend to write a book about teacher attrition, but the day I heard my friend and colleague Abby was quitting teaching, I was stunned and saddened. See, I'd watched her, smiling down the hallway, welcoming kids and parents, gliding with what seemed like ease, charm, and endless positive energy. She loved teaching. She loved the kids. They adored her and did creative, meaningful, and engaging learning with her.

But it wasn't enough.

Abby quit teaching after two years at our school and took her enthusiasm, boundless energy, creativity, and kindness with her to a job with the State of Vermont. The students were devastated, and as her mentor I felt as though I had failed her.

So I started to read and learn about teacher attrition. I learned that one in three new teachers quit after a mere three years in the profession. And the number grows to 50 percent in some areas after five years (National Commission on Teaching and America's Future [NCTAF], 2003). I started reading teacher blogs and heard similar themes and frustrations from today's new teachers.

This coincided with a tough year for me in teaching. I was not new, as I had been teaching for several years. A perfect storm of difficult parents, a new principal, and a new teaching partner brought many of these issues to the forefront for me.

I started writing about my experiences, and then I started talking to my friends and former colleagues who, like Abby, had quit teaching. I interviewed teachers from across the United States, in rural, urban, and suburban schools. Their words were compelling, vivid, and surprisingly similar. I heard many of the same themes, told in different ways. Their experiences were real, painful, and telling. I knew I had to share them.

Of course, I don't mean to imply that all great teachers quit. I know many master teachers who are still at it, 30 years later. There are thousands of amazing teachers across America educating our nation's youth. Nor do I mean to say that it is only great teachers who quit. But there is some evidence to suggest that the teachers who do make a speedy exit from teaching have a "greater measured ability," according to the Research and Development Institute (Guarino, Santibanez, Daley, & Brewer, 2004). And the one I watched leave our community was most certainly great. So yes, this is mostly subjective, but I would bet that many of the teachers who do move on are exceptional, or have the ability to become so with time and experience.

I do not claim to be an expert on teacher attrition or the current educational literature. I am merely a teacher, who has been working intensely in this field for 10 years. This book is based on my experiences and ideas, and the voices of the many teachers with whom I spoke. I wrote this book late at night after full days of teaching and parenting my two little girls. It was not easy, but I was driven by what I felt was an issue of critical importance in the education of our nation's young people.

After I started to work with Corwin, I began to solicit the experiences of teachers who are still in the field, in addition to those who have stopped teaching. This is critical because there are so many great veteran teachers in America who are still teaching, despite the ever-increasing challenges. They have developed the strategies and support mechanisms that help them make the choice to continue to teach. Their words are needed here to teach us all what great teachers and educational leaders can do to stem the tide of teachers out the door.

This is not meant to be a research-laden, academic book. It is meant to be a fresh, in-the-trenches view of what it is like to teach in America's schools, from the voices of real teachers.

I started gathering responses first on a blog called *Why Great Teachers Quit*. I had developed a short set of questions for former teachers. Without much publicity, I heard from many educators who had left the profession and had many experiences and powerful reflections to share. Then I created the blog *Why Do You Teach?* to hear from veteran teachers. The responses started pouring in from all over the country, from big cities and tiny towns, from New York to California and in between.

Many of the respondents were fellow teachers or friends of current and former colleagues. Some were family members and friends of friends. Others must have found the blogs through a Web search or a teacher forum where I posted a link. In addition to these online communications, I also had numerous phone interviews and face-to-face intensive interviews with current and former teachers from various teaching backgrounds, geographic regions, schools, and experience levels. I heard directly from teachers all across the United States.

Many teachers were not comfortable posting their thoughts on the blogs, even with the use of only their first name. Several teachers e-mailed me their detailed responses, and I was able to engage them in a dialogue about their experiences. I wanted to learn from them as much as I could, so I could personally understand their perspectives, and then glean themes to use and communicate throughout the book. The themes are presented in the book chapters; and they are, of course, overlapping and interconnected. The themes are in no way exhaustive; they are just the issues that came up repeatedly throughout my interviews, often with the most emotion and clarity. These issues are the ones I wanted to explore, to connect with my experience and perspective, and for which it seemed important to offer potential solutions.

Chapter 1 is about standardized testing and its effects. Teachers across the country explain how these high-stakes tests affect their teaching, their students, and the climate of their schools. Working conditions, ranging from violence toward teachers, old buildings, and a lack of time for eating or using the bathroom, are explored in Chapter 2. In Chapter 3, expanding expectations for teachers and the devastating effects this can have on the personal and professional lives of teachers is explored. The constant bureaucracy of public schools and its effects on creative and innovative teaching is the focus of Chapter 4. Chapter 5 is about the lack of respect for teachers and lagging compensation, two critical issues facing education today. Chapter 6 shares the perspectives of many teachers about difficult parents, and the unique, complex, and challenging situations that arise in schools on a daily basis. Administrators, as school leaders capable of changing the climate and professionalism of a school for better or worse, are the focus of Chapter 7. School boards, with their benefits and drawbacks, and the opportunities and value of teaming with teachers are explored in Chapter 8.

Each of these chapters presents a real-life scenario described to me by an interviewee (or from my personal experience and observations); a discussion of the problem with thoughts from teachers; and a list of practical, applicable recommendations for administrators and teacher leaders. These suggestions are meant to help administrators and teachers make decisions that will improve school life for the entire school community. Next, each chapter has a short section called Words of Wisdom From Veteran Teachers, which draws on the real-life experience of veteran educators and how they handle a particular issue. These suggestions were gleaned from interviews, experience, observation, and reflection. The ideas in this section are meant to be positive, forward thinking, and inspirational to teachers as they deal with these difficult issues. The chapters also share real-world stories of triumph, in Success Stories and in Hope on the Horizon, that came from my research and interviews. These are meant to show how some of these issues are being dealt with right now at the school level, with great success. Most chapters also contain a hopeful section describing why teachers teach: The Silver Lining. All chapters end with an additional resources section to give readers a place to go for more information about a particular topic. In the final chapter, I gather final thoughts for educational leaders, policy makers, and teachers.

During the writing of this book, I began reading current teacher literature that dealt with the recurring themes I was hearing in my interviews. I found many books addressing how important teachers and education are in general, and books that implore teachers and administrators to do this or that. But I rarely found books that addressed the real and pressing concerns of teachers about the state of teaching in America. A few exceptional books did provide insight and empathy for the situations teachers face in schools today. The current teacher literature I cited in this book connects the themes here and, in some cases, provides justification and elaboration in the areas where I make specific recommendations to administrators.

The purpose of this book is to give voice to the legions of hardworking, dedicated teachers across the country and to publicly recognize the challenges they face every day. Many people have no idea what it is like to be a teacher today. There are countless myths and a seemingly unending supply of misinformation about the teaching profession. Beyond gathering the thoughts of teachers, my goal is for the problems and issues they raise to be brought to the forefront in educational decision making and discussion. We need talented, motivated, and enthusiastic teachers in the classroom. Our current model simply isn't working, with up to 50 percent of teachers leaving the career in five years (NCTAF, 2003). We can and must do better. It is my hope this book will be read by administrators, superintendents, school board members, educational policy makers, teachers, and politicians alike. By bringing up these problems, and some of the possible ways to address them, it is my hope that schools across the country can reflect, plan, and act in a way that improves the lives of teachers and students in America's schools.

These are their experiences, situations, challenges, and shining lights of inspiration straight from America's teachers. We can all learn from them.

All names and geographic regions have been changed to protect the privacy of these former and current teachers. The grade level, years of experience, and type of school they work in (if given) is accurately reported. Many teachers who I interviewed were concerned that they would lose their jobs or their reputations in the schools in which they work, if their honest perceptions were quoted in this book.

In the words of Jonathan Kozol (2007a) in *Letters to a Young Teacher*, we teachers are witnesses. We need to share our experiences in order for people to notice and make changes:

> So I come back again to the need for teachers to speak out as witnesses to what they see each day before their eyes, whether they do this in the most restrained and quiet ways at schoolwide gatherings or meetings in the districts where they work or in bolder voices at the larger educational conferences and in the education journals and the mainstream media. "Witnessing" is a familiar term among the clergy of progressive and compassionate denominations. As I have said to you before, I think it ought to be the privilege, and the obligation, of our teachers, too. (pp. 193–194)

Acknowledgments

T his book would not have been possible were it not for the countless people who helped along the way. First, I want to deeply thank the many teachers who took time from their busy teaching and home lives to talk with me, post their comments, or e-mail me. I cannot mention them by name here, because I had to guarantee them complete anonymity so they could be honest and forthright in their assessments of the problems facing educators today. Over 70 teachers from across the nation communicated with me in person, by e-mail, and on the phone; and without them this book would not be possible. I also thank them for their kind words of support and encouragement about this book. Many teachers who I interviewed tolerated repeated e-mails from me with probing questions about their teaching life. They generously answered with critical analysis, candor, and thoughtfulness, which helped me take this book to the next level. For that, I am grateful. I am also grateful to my editor, Carol Collins, for working hard to help me make this book the best it can be.

The staff at Rumney Memorial School continues to inspire me with their devotion, professionalism, and enthusiasm for teaching. This is a school where compassion, excellence, and empathy create a family-like community. I want to thank my first editors and intrepid supporters, Julie Smart and Heather Robitaille. Whether it was a quick hallway exchange or a deep discussion over coffee, these two helped me develop ideas, provided contacts for interviews, and were in equal parts cheerleaders, grammar experts, and good listeners. My mom, Anne Farber, the English major, relentless reader, and quiet supporter, edited a first draft, too, and shared a much needed out-of-education perspective. I also want to thank my husband, Kurt Budliger, for enduring my late nights on the computer, my groggy mornings, and for supplying endless cups of coffee and support.

Last, I want to thank the students at Rumney Memorial School for the ways they surprise me, make me laugh, and show me the best ways to teach and reach them.

PUBLISHER'S ACKNOWLEDGMENTS

Corwin gratefully acknowledges the contributions of the following reviewers:

Nancy Marie Borie Betler, Instructional Specialist
Charlotte Mecklenburg Schools
Charlotte, North Carolina

Janie P. Edmonds, Superintendent
Mendham Schools
Mendham, New Jersey

Lori Helman, Assistant Professor
Department of Curriculum and Instruction
University of Minnesota
Minneapolis, Minnesota

Debra Rose Howell, Multiage Teacher, Grades 4 through 6
Monte Cristo Elementary
Granite Falls, Washington

Gaetane Jean-Marie, Associate Professor of Education
University of Oklahoma, Tulsa
Tulsa, Oklahoma

Mansoor Kapasi, Math Coach
Urban Education Partnership
Los Angeles Unified School District
Los Angeles, California

Deborah Long, BTSA Induction Coordinator
Merced Union High School District
Merced, California

Lauren Mitterman, Social Studies Teacher
Gibraltar Area Schools
Fish Creek, Wisconsin

Debra Eckerman Pitton, Professor of Education
Gustavus Adolphus College
St. Peter, Minnesota

Peggy Deal Redman, Director of Teacher Education and
Professor of Education
University of La Verne
La Verne, California

Joy Rose, High School Principal, Retired
Westerville, Ohio

Cathern Wildey, Adjunct Professor of Education
Southeastern University
Holiday, Florida

About the Author

 **Katy Farber** is a fifth- and sixth-grade teacher at Rumney Memorial School in Middlesex, Vermont. Prior to that, she taught fifth grade at Twinfield Union School, and environmental education at the Taconic Outdoor Education Center in Cold Spring, New York. She has a master's degree in teaching, with a specialization in science, grades seven through nine, from the State University of New York at Plattsburgh.

Katy has served as a teacher mentor, service-learning consultant, and teacher leader in her district. A documentary film by Noodlehead Network called *Is This Going to Be on the Test? Place-Based Learning: Kids Exploring Their Own Community* was created about the service-learning projects completed by her students in 2002. Katy wrote a teacher's guide to accompany this film. She is also a contributor to the book *Reading to Learn, a Classroom Guide to Reading Strategy Instruction,* published by the Vermont Strategic Reading Initiative and the Vermont Department of Education in 2004.

In the fall of 2009, Katy received an Earthwatch Educator Fellowship to participate in a 10-day science research expedition to Louisiana to survey swamps and cypress forests for the effects of climate change and extreme weather. She had the opportunity to communicate with her students via blog posts and Internet video, to engage them in real-life science research and field-based learning.

Katy is married to Kurt Budliger, a professional photographer, photography teacher, and former public school teacher. They have two daughters and live in Vermont.

Guardian

I am the guardian of your 10-year-old self

I bear witness, child one second

teenager the next

developing a sense

of what is right

what is wrong

and all in between

pushing the boundaries of childhood

like water on the levees

intense daily interactions

reading, writing, thinking

talking, laughing, brooding

until poof! you're gone

like summer in Vermont

or a flock of birds overhead

flying fast out of sight

I squint to see

the tiny dots disappear.

So when I see you in town

at the grocery store,

don't think I'm odd
because I stop in my tracks

shaken

because while I've stayed
the same in the mirror
you've gone through a
swirling metamorphosis
when I wasn't looking
you've danced, sung,
played, changed
and done more than
I'd ever known
or could teach you.
I'm looking for the relic
for the tiny piece
of your preadolescent
clumsy, shining self
searching the pictures
in my mind,
head spinning.

So when you see me
on the street
stop and say hello.
Tell me who you are now
and I will tell you
who you were then.

                    Katy Farber

Introduction

If you have time to whine and complain about something then you have the time to do something about it.

Anthony J. D'Angelo, *The College Blue Book*

When my friend and colleague quit teaching, and I had a tough school year, I knew I had to do something. I needed to channel my energy and thoughts into something productive. That is when I begin to write, research, and talk to people about the problem of teacher attrition.

I simply could not let another day go by, watching my talented colleagues leave teaching or let it completely consume their lives, to serious personal detriment. I've seen teachers, my friends, suffer serious health problems, marital issues, and mental illness as a result of some of the problems described in this book. It is not only these brilliant teachers who suffer; it is the very future, the children of our nation who take the brunt of teacher attrition and burnout.

It doesn't have to be this way. With careful planning and attention, most of these issues can be solved. This is not a diatribe of a burned-out teacher. I am still teaching and plan to continue. I love teaching. I adore the kids. This is why, over 10 years ago, I started my career being an outdoor educator, and it is why I earned my master's degree in education, and it is why I have been teaching in the classroom for the last ten years. What keeps me teaching, despite what you will read in the book? The curious, creative, bright-eyed, and downright magical kids I get to spend time with every day. And the amazing people who give their lives to working with them. You can read more about why I and many other teachers stay in this challenging, ever-changing, and meaningful profession throughout this book.

This book is an attempt to bring to the attention of the public the very solvable problems that face educators from the inside, in the real trenches, beyond political speeches and new initiatives. One of the problems I describe in this book is why your son's or daughter's favorite teacher left last year—or why that great physical education teacher took a sudden leave of absence. These issues affect all of us deeply.

This book is about the extremes—the worst-case scenarios that are driving many teachers out of the classroom. I do not mean to generalize that all schools are having these kinds of problems regularly. I have worked with many talented, caring, and wonderful principals, parents, and school board members. Their support, kindness, and comments have kept me going through the years. I've worked in supportive communities that value education. But this book is about what keeps me up at night: the persistent problems that keep presenting themselves to me in different ways. And I knew I had to do something.

It is important for me to note that this book is not about the school, district, or state I teach in. Nor is it about the administrator, superintendent, or the school board of my school or district. This book is based on my interviews of current and former teachers and on my experiences over the last 10 years in education. *Why Great Teachers Quit* should not be taken as a collective portrait of a school district, including my own. Portraits and examples of students, administrators, and teachers in this book are composites taken from many communities, many experiences, and many interviews.

This book is designed to be immediately useful to teachers, administrators, educational leaders, and lawmakers. For teachers, I hope by reading Recommendations for Administrators and Teacher Leaders in each chapter you will be able to support your administrators as they work to fix the problems that increase teacher attrition, and know what you can do as a teacher leader in your school. I hope this book provides you with some shared empathy and perspectives about teaching that you can find comfort in. I also hope that you can read Words of Wisdom From Veteran Teachers in each chapter to derive some inspiration for how to navigate these challenging problems facing educators today. Success Stories, Hope on the Horizon, and the sections about the reasons teachers teach are meant to be inspiring, uplifting, and hopeful.

One use for this book is to read and discuss it in a book-club format for educators. At our school we've done this with a few books, and it led to enriching discussions and, more important, school-wide decisions about key issues. There is much to discuss here.

For administrators, especially those without significant teaching experience, it is my hope that by reading this book you will glimpse a different perspective about teaching in America today. I hope you will see how you can make many positive changes, with just a little planning and forethought, to improve the climate, communication, safety, and morale in your school. The recommendations for administrators and teacher leaders are meant to be practical, doable steps for improving the issue discussed in each chapter. They are a starting point. Certainly, your experience and particular school community will guide you to use what makes sense for your situation.

For educational leaders and policy makers, I hope you can use this text and your position to hear the voices of teachers and apply them to any decisions you are making about education today. Too many times decisions to improve education are made by those who have never taught a day in their lives, and they simply don't understand or realize the implications of those actions. By reading this book, it is my hope that you will reflect on the challenges facing teachers today before making policy changes that might increase the problem of teacher attrition. Many of these suggestions are found in the last chapter and throughout the sections titled Recommendations for Administrators and Teacher Leaders. We cannot do this without you.

For teacher education students, I hope that this book provides you with a real-life glance into the world of teaching, so you can begin your career with your head held high, knowing what you will face, and knowing some of what you can do about it. We need your talent, enthusiasm, and excitement in teaching.

No other initiative will work unless we address these problems from the inside out. It is our moral obligation to our children to hire, train, and keep the best teachers where they belong: in the classroom, educating our future leaders.

CHAPTER ONE

Standardized Testing

> She paces the classroom during the test, not daring to sit or to carry a pen or pencil to work on some grading. Her feet ache, and she has countless things to do. Lisa thought that during the test she'd be able to catch up on her grading, to finally write back to her students in their personal journals, and plan for the next units of study in her classes. A few teachers in her school didn't follow strict test-proctoring strategies (which invalidated test scores for an entire grade), and since then, teachers have been doubted and watched closely. So she attempts to casually circulate, as her principal told her to. For two hours. She was warned to never stand still, and in no circumstance was she to speak or make a hand gesture to her students. Lisa never thought she would find herself in this situation, a creative teacher whose graduate school program focused on critical thinking and problem solving, not bubble sheets and test proctoring. She thinks about her career choice over and over, as she also wishes she had worn different shoes.

Mention No Child Left Behind, or state-mandated standardized tests, and teachers will tell you how they feel. Formal and highly structured standardized testing takes place in every public school in our nation in Grades 3 through 12. Every teacher has a reaction to this, and none are immune to the effects of standardized tests on their teaching, the climate of their schools, and the students.

EFFECTS ON SCHOOL CLIMATE

In the example above, the stressful testing scenario had a negative effect on the climate of the school. Lisa described distrust from her principal and a climate of tension and stress that permeated the whole building.

Many times, teachers are the "administrators" of these high-stakes standardized tests, usually without training or any time to review the materials and responsibilities. In addition to the regular teaching responsibilities, teachers must read and understand a 100-page booklet about the test, its administration and procedures. In many cases, they've picked up the booklet five minutes before the test, after they've sharpened 50 pencils, set up the room, put the "do not disturb" sign on the door, and turned the phone ringer off. That was after arranging for Joey to take the test in a separate space and finding breakfast for Sam, an adult to scribe for Carrie, and staff to read the questions to Steve. And now the teacher is panicked, fervently scanning the booklet for the key information. When the state monitors come to visit, those folks who know the procedures inside and out because it is their primary responsibility, they will undoubtedly find problems.

This climate of tension and stress permeates the school, not just among teachers but also among students, who were already worried about the test and now see their teacher scurrying around the room with a pinched expression.

EFFECTS ON CURRICULUM

After the test results come in, the effects on the school can be wide reaching. In one interviewee's school, their testing results came back low in writing. But it was not as cut and dried as one would think. The school was full of talented and well-taught writers. As required by the state, and indicated in best-practices techniques for teaching, the students were taught to use the writing process: Students wrote rough drafts, garnered feedback from peers and the teacher, then revised and edited, ultimately producing a piece they were very proud of (and that met state standards). Students also wrote about their reading in class journals, with a rubric to guide them and no space limit. On their state's standardized test, the students were given a genre of writing with which they were well acquainted: procedures. They had received direct instruction in procedure writing, and used the writing process, state rubrics, and student examples to develop standard-meeting procedure pieces. The only problem was the test provided just a small rectangle to write in. The students could not go outside this defined rectangle and had never experienced anything like this in their young writing lives.

The students clammed up; they didn't know what to do. The six-year veteran teacher I interviewed described seeing students physically tense up, their eyes wide as they tried to understand the format. They panicked. Some made a list of materials, as they'd been taught, and used up half of the space. Then, they only had room for one or two steps. The rectangle was full; the procedure was incomplete. Others wrote complete procedure pieces that were painstakingly small, barely legible. Others gave up and left the essay blank.

So the scores were low.

An article in the local newspaper reported that the students in this particular school scored low on writing. The principal was upset, and probably embarrassed, but any teacher in the school could have told you what happened. The test measured a certain type of writing, and a certain length, that was not taught or expected in school.

So, of course, this had to change. The school promptly began meeting, discussing, and engaging in professional development about writing. Everyone felt the pressure of "failing" in this space-limited kind of writing, which had not been valued, encouraged, or even talked about before this test.

The next year, the students took several practice tests and were ready for this kind of abbreviated writing. And indeed, the scores did improve. But what was lost? Are the students better off for learning it? They might or might not be, but these larger curricular questions can be lost in a high-stakes testing environment.

In some school districts, educational programs and institutions are on the chopping block if they don't lead to improved test scores. Recess, class meetings, and even whole subjects such as music, art, science, and history are being cut back or eliminated to focus on the only areas that are tested yearly: math and reading (see Figure 1.1). The *New York Times* (Dillon, 2006) reported on a survey by the Center for Educational Policy:

> Seventy-one percent of the nation's 15,000 school districts had reduced the hours of instructional time spent on history, music and other subjects to open up more time for reading and math. The center is an independent group that has made a thorough study of the new act and has published a detailed yearly report on the implementation of the law in dozens of districts. (para. 5)

Figure 1.1   Many school districts reported increasing time for ELA and math and decreasing time in other subjects since 2001. Social studies and science were more likely to lose minutes than recess, PE, or art.

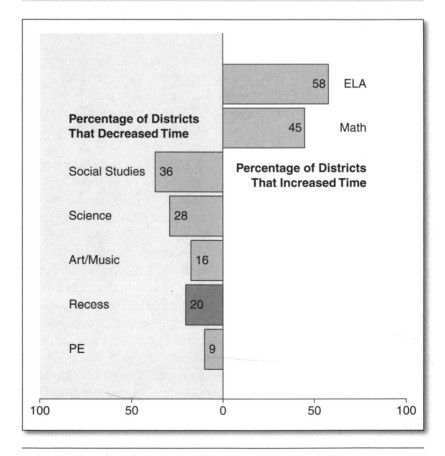

Source: Barth (2008).

For the teachers of these core subjects, they are losing their creativity and academic freedom in exchange for reading a scripted text. Elaine teaches kindergarten, and she thinks teachers need to be given more academic freedom to stay creative and engaged. About her teaching, she said, "My school uses direct instruction. Therefore, I read from a book. I act. I don't teach. I rehearse a script over and over again. It's sad." The lack of varied subjects, and rich and diverse instructional methods for teaching children, is slowly draining the life and motivation out of teaching.

EFFECTS ON TEACHING SCHEDULES AND LEARNING OUTCOMES

The standardized tests required in Grades 3 through 12 are given at different times during the school year, depending on multiple factors. Some states take the test in the fall and others in the spring. This may seem like a small item, but a great deal is affected by the testing schedule.

For example, in some western states the tests are given in May. So in the early spring, teachers are rushing through the curriculum getting students ready for these high-stakes state tests. Sam, a fourth-grade teacher, shares his perspective:

> This panic causes teachers to throw quality teaching practices out the window, and suddenly schools become stressful test-prep boot camps where dump-truck loads of concepts are crammed, jammed, and force-fed into children's minds at alarming speeds.

Struggling students who have been barely hanging on during the year may completely go under in these last few months. Many give up entirely, and this can affect their educational future for years to come.

The other disadvantage to testing in May is that the last few weeks of school (a good month or two in some schools) is considered a waste by many teachers and parents. After working so hard to get ready for the tests, many teachers cut back on expectations and teaching the curriculum, wasting valuable learning and instruction time. Without the tests to disrupt the third trimester, April, May, and early June are often prime time for student learning:

> Students are so adapted to the class that it becomes second nature; they literally soak up the knowledge and skills taught. (Teachers take it for granted, actually, how much their classes have matured and how comfortably quick the pace moves as compared to the first trimester.) It was so frustrating that other teachers (and parents, too) were sending out the message/vibe that it was "kick back" time once standardized testing had ended. The big tests have become the focus of our third trimester. Once the testing is over, it seems there is no reason to continue with the school year. It is a terrible waste of precious time that could be utilized to continue with rich and engaging lessons.

Many teachers commented on how standardized testing impacts their regular schedules and curriculum. They have been working for months to develop daily practices among their students, which benefit children academically and socially, and those are essentially thrown out for a few weeks. Losing these routines can set a class back in productivity for a great while. The testing preparation, the actual testing, and the recovery into a normal schedule can take a month or more in total. When you are only dealing with 9 or 10 months of school, this is a considerable block of time.

Consider the pressure for teachers to "finish" whatever math program they are using. Math programs are designed to take the whole year. Taking that month away increases the stress and the workload for the teacher. Quickening the pace of instruction impacts students' mastery of skills. The result can be a rush-rush mentality that detracts from the ideal learning environment and lessens the ability of teachers to complete a course of instruction to prepare kids for the next grade level. According to authors of a recent study on the effects of standardized testing in Texas, the "birthplace" of the No Child Left Behind Act, this rush-rush mentality and focus on test preparation has caused a reduction in the quality and quantity of curriculum, increased instruction of lower level skills, and has increased the gap between the poorest and most privileged children (Meier, Kohn, Darling-Hammond, Sizer, & Wood, 2004).

One of the most troubling problems with giving standardized tests for two or three weeks was shared by a special educator from a rural school:

> Most of the students I teach need intensive instruction daily to meet their IEP [Individualized Education Plan] goals, and to function well in school. During the days we are testing, all our staff is utilized by giving the tests with accommodations, so there is no time to do this crucial work with kids. They end up losing days of instruction and progress that we need to be making to help them progress. And these are the children who need structure, routine, and predictability. With days of repeated testing, all that goes out the window. With many kids, you have to start from scratch after testing. The damage is palpable, and it takes awhile for these students to get back into their instruction and routines.

This comment illustrates how testing can take up much more time than simply giving the test, especially for special education students. This teacher and others I interviewed are frustrated with how standardized testing disrupts classroom routines, curricular goals, and the progress of special education students.

EFFECTS ON STUDENTS

You may have heard about the sixth grader who was not allowed to leave his classroom during the standardized tests to use the bathroom. Then, in the classroom filled with his peers, the 12-year-old boy had an accident. Imagine the humiliation and the damage done to this boy's self image in the sixth grade, when students are in preadolescence and are very insecure. This incident, written about by Dan Brown (2007) in the *Huffington Post*, illustrates the troubling high-stakes climate in which children are facing these tests.

Many teachers I interviewed talked about the stress the daily hours of testing places on their students.

One nine-year veteran teacher talked about how developmentally inappropriate it was to ask third- and fourth-grade students to sit still and be quiet (and to masterfully take a test) for several days in a row, for two hours a day. The educator watched them read a passage again and again, trying to find the right answer, squirming, stewing, visibly quaking with energy, effort, and frustration. Their third-grade bodies just couldn't handle this type of testing, and the teacher wondered how exactly this could measure their ability, if they are not developmentally ready to show what they know on the test.

Teachers have told me of students vomiting or feeling nauseated before, during, and after the test. Others have seen repeated headaches develop in their most bright and astute students.

Many teachers discussed the troubling departure from a more rich and diverse instructional program to basic test-prep work. Students who might exceed the standard and need more in-depth learning may not get it during this time. And students who are seriously struggling might be left behind in all the flurry of test preparation.

This effect is especially pernicious for students at low-performing schools, most of them from poor urban families, who are being subjected to lower-level drill for skill-type teaching, day in and day out. These children may indeed learn how to improve their test scores, by memorizing a discreet set of facts or ideas, and not understand or comprehend them for long-term retention and the development of critical-thinking skills. Alfie Kohn (2000) writes in *Education Week*:

Again, there's no denying that many schools serving low-income children of color were second-rate to begin with. Now, however, some of these schools, in Chicago, Houston, Baltimore, and elsewhere, are arguably becoming third-rate as testing pressures lead to a more systematic use of low-level, drill-and-skill teaching, often in the context of packaged programs purchased by school districts. Thus, when someone emphasizes the importance of "higher expectations" for minority children, we might reply, "Higher expectations to do what? Bubble-in more ovals correctly on a bad test—or pursue engaging projects that promote sophisticated thinking?" The movement driven by "tougher standards," "accountability," and similar slogans arguably lowers meaningful expectations insofar as it relies on standardized testing as the primary measure of achievement. The more that poor children fill in worksheets on command (in an effort to raise their test scores), the further they fall behind affluent kids who are more likely to get lessons that help them understand ideas. If the drilling does result in higher scores, the proper response is not celebration, but outrage: The test results may well have improved at the expense of real learning. (pp. 60, 46–47)

In some cases, when it looks as though test scores are going up, one must read the back story to understand whether all students were assessed, how the dropout rate plays into it, and how much quality teaching is happening. Houston, Texas, was touted nationally as a success story for raising the test scores of all of its students. The district claimed a low 1.5 percent dropout rate, but at Sharpston High School, 463 of 1,700 students left during the school year; none were reported as dropping out. Instead, they were assigned a code that meant they had changed schools, gone back to a native country, or gone for their GED, when many of them never reported these reasons to the school (Meier et al., 2004). The real story is that a new correlation has arisen from frequent standardized testing: falling graduation rates as standardized testing increases (Meier et al., 2004).

Jonathan Kozol (2007b) also decries the effects of standardized testing on teachers and on the education that African American children in large measure are receiving. He said in the *Huffington Post* article about his hunger strike against No Child Left Behind:

When I ask them why they've grown demoralized, they routinely tell me it's the feeling of continual anxiety, the sense of being in a kind of "state of siege," as well as the pressure to conform to teaching methods that drain every bit of joy out of the hours that their children spend with them in school.

"I didn't study all these years," a highly principled and effective first-grade teacher told me—she had studied literature and anthropology in college while also having been immersed in education courses—"in order to turn black babies into mindless little robots, denied the normal breadth of learning, all the arts and sciences, all the joy in reading literary classics, all the spontaneity and power to ask interesting questions that kids are getting in the middle-class white systems." (para. 5–6)

Every year, high-stakes standardized testing wreaks havoc on student learning, school climate, and teaching in myriad ways, and the cumulative effects on schools, students, and teachers cannot be understated.

you can... **DO IT!** RECOMMENDATIONS FOR ADMINISTRATORS AND TEACHER LEADERS

- During an inservice at the beginning of the year, discuss with staff the testing practices, schedule, and policies of the school. Providing this framework allows teachers to look at their curricular plans and maps to see how testing will fit in. Then teachers can plan around this timetable and anticipate the impact to their curriculum. While these ideas are best practice, and written into legislation in some states, it is doubtful that they happen regularly in all schools.

- Provide training for teachers and school staff on test administration. Staff meetings are a great time for this, so teachers do not have to use their planning or personal time to prepare for the test. This could be as simple as providing time for teacher teams to read and review the testing protocols for each grade level. It is helpful if this is done a few weeks in advance of the test, so teachers and school staff have some time to address any gaps or problems in the procedural expectations for the exam. That way, administrators know their staff has been prepared for the testing, and can have trust and faith in their ability to proctor it.

- Provide time and opportunity for teachers and special educators to meet and review the testing needs for various students. This can eliminate hurried hallway consultations about where a child who needs a separate testing environment will work.

- Develop strategies with the guidance counselor for how to prepare students for the testing environment, especially for elementary students. Guidance counselors can team with teachers to help prepare students for this testing, or the guidance counselor can teach a few classes about handling test anxiety.

- Team up to send information home about how parents can support their child during the test-taking period. There is lots of good information about this available, and it can make all the difference for students. See the additional resources section on page 17.

- Communicate the value of student's education beyond the test scores to teachers and staff. This will help teachers see that administrators don't view tests as the end-all-be-all of education and that they care about the whole child as well, not just the snapshot the test provides.

- Collaborate with states to determine the testing window. It would be beneficial for states, administrators, teachers, and educational leaders to agree on a schedule that will have the least negative impact on students and quality teaching. This decision should not be based on how much it will cost (as it is in some states) but on the best time for teachers and students.

- Encourage teachers to prepare students for the format of the tests. By looking at the actual format in a practice test, students are much more at ease when the actual tests come around, as are teachers. And more of what they know will be shared in the test. This doesn't mean teaching to the test, or doing weeks of test preparation, but allowing students to become familiar with the format so they aren't overwhelmed in the moment.

WORDS OF WISDOM FROM VETERAN TEACHERS

When asked how to cope with the pressures of standardized testing, veteran teachers try to put it in perspective. They know that these scores do not reflect everything they do with their students, and it never could. Many teachers advocate for more classroom-based measures of success.

Veteran teachers also do not seem to throw out the regular curriculum for test preparation. They integrate it into their teaching throughout the year or do only a few sessions to prepare their kids for the strategies and format of the test. They believe in their teaching and their students enough to avoid getting swept up in the drama of standardized testing.

Teachers also have been rallying and organizing around this issue. They have made recommendations for how to change the

No Child Left Behind Act to include a greater focus on classroom-based assessments. They will undoubtedly be influencing future legislation in the current administration. Veteran teachers advocate, write, and speak up on these issues and encourage others to do so, too. As Kozol (2007a, p. 207–208) in *Letters to a Young Teacher* puts it, teachers need to "see themselves not just as skilled practitioners but also as warriors for justice. If they won't speak out for their kids, who will?"

THE SILVER LINING: PERSONALLY FULFILLING

Sophie is finishing the dishes. It's after 8 p.m., and she's tired; she's been on her feet teaching all day, then chasing around her young children after school. Her mind wanders to her former student, Liz, who is about to go in for knee surgery. She picks up the phone and calls her.

They talk, really talk, about knees, recovery, books, and school. Having an adult to talk to—who is not one of your parents—is a big deal, and the tension in Liz's voice eases a bit through the conversation. Liz thanks Sophie, and they hang up.

This is why Sophie teaches. It's the meaningful interactions between herself and her students, sometimes years after having taught them, that keep her going.

Sophie is like so many teachers I have spoken with. She started teaching because she loved being with children and wanted to make a difference in their lives. Now, when faced with standardized tests, endless standards, and increasing paperwork, she remembers these relationships. They are what matters most.

Sophie's feelings were echoed by many teachers. A teacher from an urban high school said, "I just can't seem to find anything else that is as satisfying and fulfilling as teaching. There is *no* other job that lets you make such a huge difference in so many people's lives."

She is reflecting not on the limited tangible rewards, of course, but on the personal connections a teacher can make with students. This might never be spoken. That feeling of fulfillment might come from only a nod, a smile, or knowing that a child is safe, has learned something, or developed confidence because of you. These are not measured by tests, but their impact can be monumental.

HOPE ON THE HORIZON: REEVALUATING OUR STANDARDIZED-TESTING CULTURE

Thankfully, many teachers, educational writers, professors, principals, and administrators are sounding the alarm about the damage that high-stakes testing is having on our nation's children, our teachers, and our schools. Principal George Wood encourages those involved with education:

> Educators, parents, and students need to come together to challenge what is happening to the daily quality of school life for our children as a result of the pressure on testing. We seem to have accepted these tests as a fact of life when in fact they are only a recent development with no proven history. And now we have for the first time a federal law that mandates this unproven measure of our schools as the arbiter of what counts as a quality education. (Meier et al., 2004, p. 48)

He and the other authors of *Many Children Left Behind* offer real, meaningful, and doable suggestions for how to modify our national education strategy and plan. These ideas include more flexibility with how to assess students at different developmental levels, using multiple measures for assessment, looking at the overall progress of a student versus a snapshot that testing provides, among other suggestions.

We are coming through a time period with singular and heavy focus on regular standardized testing. We've seen the results. Now it is time for a more moderate, thoughtful, and measured approach that values the opinions of teachers, parents, administrators, and students as much as politicians and educational experts.

ADDITIONAL RESOURCES

Print Resources

Flippo, R. (2008). *Preparing students for testing and doing better in school.* Thousand Oaks, CA: Corwin.

Kohn, A. (2000). *The case against standardized testing: Raising the scores, ruining the schools.* Portsmouth, NH: Heinemann.

McNeil, L. (2007). *Contradictions of school reform: Educational costs of standardized testing.* London: Taylor & Francis.

Myers, E. (2009). *The power of teacher networks.* Thousand Oaks, CA: Corwin.

Sack, P. (2001). *Standardized minds: The high price of America's testing culture and what we can do to change it.* Cambridge, MA: Da Capo Press.

Internet Resources

General Test Tips for Helping Your Child During This Stressful Time

Family Education. (n.d.). *Standardized tests: Preparation and advice.* Available from http://school.familyeducation.com/educational-testing/study-skills/34555.html

Links to Articles and Books Recommended by PBS About Helping Your Child With Standardized Testing

PBS Parents. (n.d.). *It's my life: Test stress.* Available from http://pbskids.org/itsmylife/parents/resources/teststress.html

Tips for Parents to Help Children With Differing Learning Styles

Molland, J. (n.d.). *How to help all kids succeed on standardized tests.* Available from www.parenthood.com/article-topics/how_to_help_all_kids_succeed_on_standardized_tests.html

Steps for Teachers, Parents, Administrators, School Board Members, and Superintendents to Fight the Overuse of Standardized Testing in Schools

Kohn, A. (2001, January). Fighting the tests: A practical guide to rescuing our schools. *Phi Delta Kappan.* Available from www.alfiekohn.org/teaching/ftt.htm

CHAPTER TWO

Working Conditions in Today's Schools

Frank's day started like any other. After teaching for over 30 years in inner-city Philadelphia, he knew how to get the high school students' attention to begin class. But on this particular day, one student wouldn't turn off his iPod. Frank asked him again and said he would have to take it away if he didn't turn it off. The last thing he remembers is the student putting his iPod on the desk. Frank thought the confrontation was over.

Within minutes, Frank was unconscious on the floor, his blood pooling around him, and his neck broken. Turns out, Frank had asked to speak to the boy in the hall, where the assault began. The boy pushed him from behind and began driving his head into a locker. Frank ended up with five broken bones in his neck and traumatic brain injury.

We know that the educational system is broken in many inner cities (and in many American schools) for teachers and students. It can be unsafe for everyone. Some kids are hungry, scared, and barely surviving and certainly not learning. This has been written about extensively, especially by advocates and educational writers such as Jonathan Kozol. The following chapter is about the effects of this complex problem, and other problems with working conditions in schools, on teacher attrition and attitudes.

Source: National Public Radio (NPR), Burd, & Cline (2007).

BIG PROBLEM #1: VIOLENCE

Frank's story was not the only serious teacher assault in 2007 in inner-city Philadelphia. Ed Cline, a 16-year teaching veteran, was forced to move schools after only one month of the school year because his school dropped their music program. His new school was "utter chaos," as he described it (NPR, Burd, & Cline, 2007). After repeated incidents, threats, and intimidation, he was attacked by a student and received a broken jaw and a severe concussion. These two extreme situations were in high-poverty, urban schools where the teachers and staff were constantly overwhelmed, threatened, and intimidated.

And they are not alone. Teachers around the United States feel threatened and are assaulted as they work in the areas where we need them most: underperforming schools where both poverty and dropout rates are high. In response to the two Philadelphia assaults, many urban teachers posted comments on the Edweek blog. Here is what one teacher had to say about her situation:

> I have been teaching for 28 years. Within the last 7 years I have experienced 3 incidents of physical assault by students, 1 incident of physical fondling by 6 male students and 7 threats with intent to do bodily harm. We have no support from the administration and the Chicago Teachers Union does little to support this. I have contemplated starting a coalition to support teachers/educators that have had such experiences. My close friends and other colleagues have either left the teaching profession or left our school because of the acts of violence by students against them. (As it first appeared in the Around the Web blog on www.edweek.org, June 27, 2007. Reprinted with permission from Education Week.)

Clearly the violence and intimidation in these schools is driving teachers away, in challenging, already hard-to-staff schools. Another inner-city high school teacher told her story:

> I actually had a parent stalking the parking lot every morning, wanting to talk to me about her "precious" whose grade was slipping because she wasn't attending my class, and

when she did attend, she didn't do anything. I wrote a complaint to our administration, because I felt my safety was at stake, and absolutely NOTHING was done to provide it.

So many laws that protect everyone except teachers. We are the real victims at times, and that's because it's acceptable to administrators. If they aren't protecting us, who will?

Are they waiting until murder is taking place in the classroom to enforce something? Parents, wake up and help us out here. Don't you want your kid to learn something other than how the teacher has to handle the unruly? Standards, Standards, Standards. Who has the time to teach them with so much management taking place? (As it first appeared in the Around the Web blog on www.edweek.org, June 27, 2007. Reprinted with permission from Education Week.)

Teachers, students, and administrators are deeply affected by school violence at all grade levels. The literature is rich with the causes, problems, and effects of violence and poverty in inner-city schools. And there are many good people trying to improve the situation. But the obvious fact remains that teacher attrition will be higher in schools with chronic violence and a volatile climate (Flood & Anders, 2005), and this must change to keep our good teachers where they are needed most. The situation is compounded by the misinformed practice of assigning new teachers the most difficult classes in these settings.

One teacher in inner-city Pittsburgh shared how a student defecated and smeared it on the walls and door of her classroom. There was no janitor in the school, and she had to clean it up herself, risking her health and certainly her mental well-being. The impact of this one act could have enormous effects on this teacher's future in the career. This same teacher had been pushed and threatened. She even revealed a student plot to kill students and teachers. In each case, she was not supported by the administration, nor were the students given any consequences or suspensions. This teacher took the first opportunity to teach in a private school with more support and resources, leaving behind an unsafe, violent, and depressed school. Like many teachers, through no fault of their own, she left for a better job. The kids are the ones who pay the price for this flight.

Students at Risk for Violent Behavior

- History of being violent toward his/her peers
- Access to firearms
- Involved in drinking alcohol or taking other drugs
- Caregivers have a history of drug/alcohol involvement
- Peer group reinforces antisocial behaviors
- Learned attitudes accepting aggressive behaviors as "normal" and an effective way to solve problems
- High level of violence in the home, in the neighborhood, and in the media
- School history that includes aggressive and disruptive classroom behavior
- Poor school achievement, poor school attendance, and numerous school suspensions
- Difficulty with social skills and poor peer relations
- Difficulty controlling his/her impulses and emotions
- History of parental rejection, inconsistent discipline, and lack of supervision

Source: Teachers First and National Association of School Psychologists (n.d., para. 1).

BIG PROBLEM #2: UNSAFE SCHOOLS

Every spring in a suburban elementary school, music teacher Carla would get a case of chronic bronchitis. Her throat would hurt, and her voice would become raspy. She usually just dealt with it, and chalked it up to her close contact with over a hundred children on a daily basis.

Then early in one school year, her sore throat and raspy voice came on and didn't go away. She tried every trick in the book, lozenges, tea, gargling, and it got worse and worse. Then she started to have trouble breathing.

Carla finally complained to her administrators, who told her to move her classroom (which of course is no easy task). She did, but her symptoms did not improve.

Carla split her time between two schools teaching elementary music. When she left for her duties at the other school, her problems would ease. As soon as she returned, her symptoms would resurface, with a vengeance.

She started missing school because she felt so sick. When she would reenter the building, her symptoms would flare up so dramatically she would have to leave immediately or suffer labored breathing.

Carla's doctor told her to quit working at the school—that going to the school was detrimental to her health. All the while, she was missing school and using up her sick days.

She went into the office to discuss the situation with her two principals. One accused her of not caring about the children (because she was missing so much school) and told her she needed to come to work.

Carla responded, "I built the whole music program in this school from nothing. I have great reviews. I love the students. This is not about them."

After this troubling meeting, Carla started organizing with other teachers who were suffering health problems because of the indoor air quality at their school. Several teachers got in touch with Carla and shared their own stories about sinus infections, headaches, and breathing problems. Some were taking steroids and antibiotics regularly. They met with the National Education Association and discussed filing a lawsuit.

Meanwhile, Clara kept missing school and waiting for her sick time to run out. It didn't. The school kept paying her. All the while, the children in the school were exposed to poor air quality daily, with their young and developing bodies more vulnerable than adults.

The next year, Carla was transferred to a different school. The mold problem at her old school went on for years. Years of children and adults suffering from poor air quality at a place they came to work and learn.

Carla said, "Isn't my health valued as a teacher? And what about the kids? They never really fixed it. The kids still suffer today."

Walking hand in hand with violence is another big problem: the broken-down, outdated, and unsafe physical condition of school buildings. Many of our nation's schools are old and decaying, causing health problems for the teachers and students who inhabit them on a daily basis. Carla's story is only one example of the working conditions that are literally harming teachers and students.

Schools across the country, many in urban areas, are in a chronic state of disrepair, with broken fire alarms and nonworking intercoms (Flood & Anders, 2005). They are dark, dingy, and depressing. In addition to being unsafe, these conditions create a negative climate for teachers and students that is not conducive to learning. Although they can be expensive to address, schools need to take these issues very seriously to protect the well-being of all people in our public schools.

An inner-city teacher, Avalon (2007), had this to say about the impact of a building's safety on school climate:

> Building conditions have a HUGE impact on school climate and safety. I've personally tried to inform administrators of broken locks/cameras/doors/intercoms/alarms. They don't get fixed, at least not in a timely manner, and repeated attempts to have the problems fixed are met with the clear indication that we are being unreasonable pests. Some of the breakdown seems to be at the school level, some at North Ave. Someone will have to get injured for anything to be done. (para. 1)

Anyone who has been in education for an extended period of time knows how long it takes to get any small repair done. Many schools are often understaffed with janitors, and communication seems to move at a glacial pace (Brodeur, 2008). This is endlessly frustrating and in many cases dangerous.

Even in more affluent schools, problems with heating, mice, leaks, and mold plague older buildings and their inhabitants (see Table 2.1). In a small rural and suburban school, one principal wouldn't turn the heat on until the end of October, no matter what, to save heating costs. This was in a northeast state, where it snows in October. The children wore their coats all day, and their lips were blue. How can these children (and teachers) learn while they are freezing?

Table 2.1 Percentage distribution of public elementary and secondary schools indicating the extent to which various environmental factors interfered with the ability of the school to deliver instruction in school buildings, by type of building: Fall 2005

Environmental Factor, by Type of Building	Not at All	Minor Extent	Moderate Extent	Major Extent	Not Applicable
Permanent buildings					
All factors, taken together	56	33	9	1	–
Artificial lighting	76	18	5	1	–
Natural lighting	73	18	5	1	3
Heating	63	24	10	3	1
Air conditioning	46	21	10	6	17
Ventilation	66	22	8	3	–
Indoor air quality	69	21	7	3	–
Acoustics or noise control	61	27	9	3	–
Physical condition of ceilings, floors, walls, windows, doors	71	19	8	3	–
Size or configuration of rooms	64	23	9	4	–

(Continued)

Table 2.1 (Continued)

Environmental Factor, by Type of Building	Not at All	Minor Extent	Moderate Extent	Major Extent	Not Applicable
Portable buildings					
All factors, taken together	55	30	13	2	–
Artificial lighting	68	25	5	3	–
Natural lighting	62	26	7	1	4
Heating	66	23	7	2	1
Air conditioning	63	22	7	4	3
Ventilation	62	24	11	3	–
Indoor air quality	62	26	10	2	–
Acoustics or noise control	56	26	14	4	–
Physical condition of ceilings, floors, walls, windows, doors	60	26	11	3	–
Size or configuration of rooms	58	26	11	5	–

– Not available

Source: National Center for Education Statistics (2007).

SMALL PROBLEMS THAT ADD UP

Sarah has had to go to the bathroom for hours. She's been teaching straight from 7:30 to 12, and she is squirming, trying to concentrate on her eighth graders' narrative writing pieces. Sarah looks at the clock and weighs her options. She could leave the class unattended, and have a possible behavior problem when she returns. Thoughts of a recent news story of two fifth-graders having sex in an unsupervised classroom run through her mind. She could go to the neighboring classroom and ask him to leave his class unattended. None of these are viable options, so she soldiers on, minute by minute. Sarah is five months pregnant, and she is barely making it to her first break of the day. She knows this can't be good for her or for the baby.

The above scenario takes place in countless schools across America today, whether the teacher is pregnant or not. Teachers teach for hours on end, with the schedule usually dictated by the numbers of students, course offerings, teacher availability, and state requirements. All of these are very important, of course. But so are the very basic physical needs of teachers.

Take lunch, for example. In my interviews, a few teachers pointed out that a lack of time for eating and using the bathroom could be another reason to select a different career path. Eating and using the bathroom should not be stressful activities, but teachers commented that these times usually amounted to less than 30 minutes a day and were very rushed. Often teachers would eat while grading, preparing lessons, serving or monitoring lunch, or while talking about a student issue with another staff person in the hallway. None of this is good for the health and well-being of the people who teach our children.

One urban teacher put it this way: "Most workers get one hour for lunch. Teachers *may* get 30 to 40 minutes depending on your school." The Teachers Net chat board shares this story (Ms. Pickle, 2006):

I just moved here and do not get a 30-minute duty free lunch period! Eekk!! I go to lunch at 11:05. My kids get their lunch by 11:15 and seated. They dismiss them at 11:25. TEN MINUTES!!!

I don't get to eat, because I have to help them wash hands, get in line, and get seated. I have lost 6 pounds in 12 days. This may be good for some, but now I weigh 98 pounds and am exhausted by the afternoon. Is this normal for Louisiana? They don't follow the federal mandated duty free lunch? (para. 1)

After reading this comment, can you imagine why she might not want to stay in teaching? It seems like a small, simple thing, but it is one issue in a fragile and highly built deck of cards. And unfortunately, there is no federally mandated duty-free lunch for teachers.

The working conditions for educators across the nation vary widely. Some problems are arguably just too big for administrators and the school community to solve alone, but many of these issues, such as providing sufficient time for lunch, can be improved or eliminated with good planning and action throughout the school year.

RECOMMENDATIONS FOR ADMINISTRATORS AND TEACHER LEADERS

- There are many schools and districts where educators and administrators have developed extensive programs and plans to improve school safety. In addition, many nonprofit organizations and government agencies share information and support to schools. Specific recommendations and information from these groups are included in the additional resources section.

- Develop a school-safety task force including the custodian, a school board member, a teacher, and the principal. This team can survey the school (and the teachers and students) to determine what needs attention to make the school a safer place. Then all parties can work together, with specific timelines and progress check-ins to make sure the work happens in a timely manner. This work should be a priority. Examples of surveys are in the additional resources section at the end of this chapter.

- Work closely with teachers and guidance counselors to identify children at risk of violent behavior, and look into options to support these students in any way possible (community organizations, alternative programs, mentoring, counseling). The school team can closely monitor these students and make connections with and for them. This is crucial for preventing school violence.

- Develop a child-safety committee that meets weekly or biweekly to proactively address students with extra needs (hunger, neglect, isolation, and emotional and behavioral concerns). This could be one of the major committee commitments for staff during the year. Ideally, the school nurse, guidance counselor, special educator, and any teaching staff working with a particular student of concern should attend.

- Develop an explicit school emergency plan to address dangerous situations (student with a gun, or an intruder). Practice the protocols with the staff and work out any potential glitches. There are many resources to assist with this process, and several are listed at the end of this chapter.

- The entire school staff should take every threat and act of intimidation from students to teachers seriously. The administrators should follow up with parent communication and consequences for the student.

- Utilize the local police department for support, as well, in any school safety situation.

- If your school is prone to violence, provide or seek meaningful training for all school staff about how to handle threats and acts of physical violence. Courses and workshops are usually available at regional universities. As a school, develop procedures for what to do when students fight or threaten each other. Make this part of the school safety plan, and review it with staff before the school year so everyone is prepared.

- In high-violence schools, provide teachers with a weekly or monthly check-in time (during school hours) to discuss the strategies they use to keep kids and teachers safe.

- Explain to the school staff any mental health benefits available through your school's insurance or have insurance representatives do a presentation about this. A school nurse or the guidance counselor may also be knowledgeable in this area and know where to direct school staff. Be knowledgeable about where to direct teachers affected by threats and acts of violence.

- A team of teachers, administrators, and the school nurse can start an environmental health and safety committee. It should involve a yearly air quality and safety survey from an outside organization, who can deliver an unbiased report about the school's needs. Then this report should be shared with the teachers and school community. This group can develop action steps to improve the current climate for everyone. Surveys can also be sent home to determine teacher and student health and well-being. Then prompt action can be taken to correct threats to everyone's health within the school. School environmental health surveys and resources are listed at the end of this chapter (see Additional Resources).

- To limit exposure to chemicals, this team can replace toxic cleaners with greener options that are safer for everybody. According to the Vermont Public Interest Group, one high school saw a 33 percent drop in headaches, nausea, and asthma issues after the school started using less-toxic cleaning products (Hinckley, 2008).

- Complaints about air quality and occupational safety should be taken very seriously and acted upon. Administrators (along with the environmental health and safety team) can be supportive and considerate by listening to the problem and offering timely solutions to address the area of concern and protect everyone.

- Everyone deserves a duty-free lunch, and veteran teachers encourage others to advocate for this in their contract negotiations, if it is not part of their contract already. Make it a contractual right. Of course, teachers also have to advocate for themselves by not scheduling meetings during that time and by reminding administrators that they need to have some time to eat. Teachers can also support each other in this by encouraging staff to eat together and relax for a few minutes to regroup (as long as this can stay positive and productive for the school climate).

- Administrators can advocate for their staff to have a duty-free lunch by not scheduling meetings during that time or expecting teachers to handle discipline infractions and follow-up during this time.

• Teachers can improve working conditions by speaking up. Show your administrators your dirty classroom, unsafe areas, or mold problems. Encourage strongly that it be fixed in a timely manner. If it isn't, talk to the school board, superintendent, and possibly community organizations for assistance. According to the book *Motivating and Inspiring Teachers*, by Todd and Beth Whitaker, and Dale Lumpa (2000), a clean, organized, safe school is most likely a positive, successful one, which everyone wants. If no action is taken, and the area is unsafe, take pictures of the area and write down any health or other problems associated with it. Having a record will be helpful if you need to get anyone else involved. There are many government, nonprofit, and environmental health organizations that can offer steps for schools, parents, and teachers to take to improve the situation.

• One way staff can support each other having a few minutes to use the bathroom is to advocate for this in the school planning and scheduling. Many folks to do not realize that teachers are responsible for their students for over three hours at a time with no bathroom breaks. Some education around this during scheduling will help everyone understand and plan for solutions that work for everyone. If a schedule is already in place, teachers can work together with support staff to schedule times during the day where students can be supervised by someone else for a few minutes. These are a few strategies that worked for some of the teachers I interviewed and others I have worked with.

• When scheduling classes, administrators (or a scheduling committee) can look at the hours of teaching time and student supervision for each teacher to determine where teachers might need a quick bathroom break (usually every two hours). Then they can work with support staff to schedule short breaks for teachers as needed.

• One group particularly vulnerable to teacher attrition is breastfeeding mothers of babies (National Center for Education Statistics, 2008). These women need a bit more time for breaks during the school day if they are breastfeeding and need to express milk during the day. To promote this healthy way of feeding babies, schools can develop strategies and procedures to support working mothers, thus helping them be more likely to continue teaching as new parents. These can include providing coverage in their classes during times when a mother needs to pump milk, and a quiet, private place to do so, behind a door that can be locked.

The Benefits of Supporting Breastfeeding Mothers at Work

Why support nursing moms in your workplace? Because it's worth it. With a few months of flexibility, your business reaps tremendous rewards:

- Fewer sick days for moms
  - Formula feeding moms have three times as many one-day absences from work to care for sick children in the first year of life than do breastfeeding moms. Cohen, Mrtek, and Mrtek (1995)
  - It is estimated that, for every 1000 formula feeding babies, their mothers would miss a total of one full year of employment in excess of breastfeeding mothers, because their children are sick so much more often. Ball and Wright (1999)
- Return on your investment
  - Aetna found a $2.8 return for every $1 invested to support lactation.
  - Sanvita, a worksite lactation support company, has found that companies have obtained $1.50 to $4.50 for each dollar invested.
- Lower health care costs
  - Infants who receive only their mothers' milk for the first three months of life incur $331 less in health care costs over the first year of life.
- Lower staff turnover
  - Employers find that lactation support leads to improved staff productivity and loyalty, helping you retain talented employees.
- Positive image of a family friendly employer

Source: Massachusetts Breastfeeding Coalition (2008).

WORDS OF WISDOM
FROM VETERAN TEACHERS

Frank Burd, who suffered in the 2007 Philadelphia attack, was amazed at the outpouring of support and emotion during his recovery. More people than he could ever have imagined came up to him and told him that they "couldn't take it" and that they had quit teaching because of the violence, the intimidation, and the lack of support and safety.

But Frank also shared how many students helped him that awful day. From the student who called 911, to the students who were on the floor to help him, and the countless students who sent him e-mails and letters of support and kindness. Students and former students told him how much his teaching made a difference in their lives. Teachers don't usually receive this kind of feedback, unless in a dramatic situation such as this. Frank said he will never leave education. He says he would miss the kids. He loves education and teaching, despite what happened to him. And we can all take inspiration from that.

What keeps schools safe are the people working in them. They know the students the best and are the ones on the front line to notice and help when a student is in trouble. By learning about children, their home lives, their interests, their personalities, teachers help keep everyone safe. Sadly, this doesn't always happen. Every day, though, teachers wake up in the morning and try to connect with students and help them with whatever they are facing. In this way, they are working to keep school communities safe.

Teacher Vicki Cox (2004) knows this. She worked in a broken-down Missouri High School, where a few days before the school year ended, a call came in stating, "The last day of school, someone is going to die." On the day of the year that is supposed to be a celebration, police monitored the grounds, the parking lot, and the school.

Then, halfway through the morning, Nick tapped me on the shoulder. I looked into a smile that spread from ear to ear. His pleasure lit the entire room. He laid a package, large enough for a weapon and long enough for a bomb, on my desk. Under the paper I carefully unfolded lay a single delicate white rose.

(Continued)

(Continued)

Nick had been one of my problem sixth graders. He had been a tight little rosebud himself, all wound up in his own world. He was determined to finish assignments first, impatient with classmates who were still working. He was the loudest and most righteous in class discussions. He lost his temper and dissolved into tears when confronted.

He and I had many conversations in the hall about his behavior. His mother and I conferenced over the phone and face to face, strategizing how to open his attention to the other students' ideas and feelings. We were patient. We were firm. We were kind. Little by little, he blossomed. He read library books while others worked. He learned not to blurt out comments, not to contradict me, and not to interrupt others. His classmates elected him student council representative. He applied, and was accepted, as a student office aide.

No test score recorded his progress, but on that day, dirtied by apprehension, he was giving me a beautiful flower. . . . Nick's last day of school ended without incident. No bombs went off. No guns were fired. Students boarded yellow buses and drove into their summer. I cleared my desk, picked up my rose, and left. When I got home, I found my most expensive vase. Nick's flower deserved my best. It stayed on my dining room table opening wide and wide, as delicate and luminous as the wafer moon. (Cox, 2004, pp. 14–15)

If we have patience, kindness, and are firm, like Vicki and Nick's mom, we can help a child change direction. More and more teachers will have the opportunity to do just that if we can improve our schools working environments to allow students, parents, and teachers to develop these important, life-changing relationships. Our students and teachers deserve safe, green, and healthy schools to learn in. It is within our grasp.

 ## HOPE ON THE HORIZON: CITIES ADOPT THE PRECAUTIONARY PRINCIPLE

Rather than waiting for crises to occur, a proactive approach to addressing the issues of children's environmental health and the ecological impacts of schools can be based on the *precautionary principle*.

A growing number of cities, including San Francisco, have adopted the precautionary principle as guidance for a range of decisions to promote environmental health and safety, to reduce costs, and to promote sustainability in government practices, including switching to nontoxic cleaners and environmentally sound purchasing.

The Los Angeles Unified School District adopted the precautionary principle as the foundation for its decision to provide the safest, least toxic approach to pest problems after children exposed to chemical herbicides suffered serious asthma attacks.

The approach taken by these districts includes these guidelines:

- Take anticipatory action to prevent harm;
- Place the burden of proof on the proponent of a potentially harmful activity;
- Examine a full range of alternatives;
- Provide relevant communities with the right to know about potential harm; and
- Consider all the reasonably foreseeable costs of an activity. (Green Schools Initiative, n.d.)

SUCCESS STORIES: GREEN SCHOOLS

More and more schools are now analyzing their environmental impacts, often lead by students and parents, and are working toward becoming healthy, greener schools. The data supports them. In schools that have implemented programs and procedures such as the Tools for Schools Program by the Environmental Protection Agency (EPA, 2007), there have been stunning results in the health and well-being of their school staff and students.

Several schools in Connecticut used the EPA's (2007) Tools for Schools (TFS) Program and resources to improve the indoor air quality (IAQ) of their schools. This program has resources for school administrators, parents, teachers, students, and the media. The indoor air quality program, according to the EPA's (2010) website, has been implemented successfully in tens of thousands of schools nationwide. In these schools, more learning can take place because the staff and students are healthier. These tools are available to all teachers, administrators, and parents from the

EPA's Tools for Schools Program, listed in the additional resources section. All schools can work together with their communities to make their schools safer for students and more sustainable for the future of our environment.

Here are some eye-opening results from Connecticut schools using the EPA's Tools for Schools Program:

Waterford School

- Reduction of 74% in the number of IAQ health complaints in one elementary school, from 152 to 40 the year after TFS was implemented
- Decrease in IAQ health complaints of 66% or greater in 9 out of 13 elementary classrooms which was representative of the other district schools

Hamden School

- Absenteeism cut by more than half after TFS was implemented in one elementary school, from 484 days to 203 days in one year
- Marked decrease in the use of student inhalers
- Fewer complaints from staff and students of headaches and sinus infections

North Haven School

- Decrease of 48% (256) in number of reported cases of respiratory-related illnesses
- Number of clinic visits decreased by 4,978 (11%) two years after TFS was implemented

Chester School

- Number of asthma-related health office visits decreased dramatically over a period of 4 years from 463 before TFS to 82 after major TFS recommendations implemented
- Decrease in health office visits related to headaches, dizziness, and sinus difficulties (students and staff)
- Decrease in absenteeism each year

Hartford School

- Number of asthma incidents declined 21.2%, from 11,334 to 8929 in one year, after TFS was implemented in most schools
- Improvements to school buildings that included carpet replaced with tile, elimination of area rugs, repair of leaking pipes, new roofs and roof repairs, and cleaning boiler rooms

Source: Environmental Protection Agency (2007).

ADDITIONAL RESOURCES

Print Resources

Barton, E. (2006). *Bully prevention: Tips and strategies for school leaders and classroom teachers* (2nd ed.). Thousand Oaks, CA: Corwin.

Barton, E. (2009). *Leadership strategies for safe schools* (2nd ed.). Thousand Oaks, CA: Corwin.

Brunner, J., & Lewis, D. (2009). *Safe & secure schools: 27 strategies for prevention and intervention.* Thousand Oaks, CA: Corwin.

Bridgett, L. (2007). *A guide to green school success: A Maryland initiative.* St. Laurent, Quebec, Canada: Beaver Books.

Kozol, J. (1992). *Savage inequalities: Children in America's schools.* New York: Harper.

Kozol, J. (1996). *Amazing grace: Lives of children and the conscience of a nation.* New York: Harper.

National School Safety Center. (2006). *What if? Preparing schools for the unthinkable.* Westlake Village, CA: Author.

Waterman, S. S. (2006). *Four most baffling challenges for teachers and how to solve them: Classroom discipline, unmotivated students, underinvolved or adversarial parents, and tough working conditions.* Larchmont, NY: Eye on Education.

Internet Resources

Planning Guide for Maintaining School Facilities

National Center for Education Statistics. (2003). *Planning guide for maintaining school facilities* (NCES 2003-347). Available from http://nces.ed.gov/pubs2003/2003347.pdf

National School Safety Center

> National School Safety Center. (n.d.). Available from www.schoolsafety.us

Creating Safe Schools Guide

> National School Safety Center. (1999). *Working together to create safe schools.* Available from www.schoolsafety.us/pubfiles/working_together.pdf

School Safety Plan Samples and Templates

> Imperial County Office of Education. (n.d.). *School safety plans.* Available from www.icoe.k12.ca.us/ICOE/Departments/SWB/SCHOOL+SAFETY+PLANS/SCHOOL+SAFETY+PLANS.htm

School Safety Resources

> ASCD. (n.d.). *School safety resources.* Available from http://ascd.org/research_a_topic/Education_Topics/School_Safety/School_Safety_intro.aspx

> Teachers First & National Association of School Psychologists. (n.d.). *Safe schools resources.* Available from www.teachersfirst.com/crisis/resources.htm

School Safety Surveys

> Catholic Mutual Group. (n.d.). *School safety survey.* Available from www.diobr.org/documents/sch_safety_survey.pdf

> Educational and Community Supports, University of Oregon. (n.d.). *School safety survey.* Available from www.pbssurveys.org/pages/SafetySurvey.aspx

School Safety Checklist

> Teach Safe Schools. (n.d.). *School safety checklist.* Available from www.teachsafeschools.org/school-safety-checklist.html

Seven Steps to a Safer School

> Teach Safe Schools. (n.d.). *Seven steps to a safer school.* Available from www.teachsafeschools.org/seven-steps.html (with resources about putting together a safety team and plan)

Lead and Manage My School: Emergency Planning, Office of Safe and Drug-Free Schools

> Office of Safe and Drug-Free Schools. (2009). *Lead & manage my school: Emergency planning.* Available from www2.ed.gov/admins/lead/safety/emergencyplan/index.html

> National School Safety Center. (n.d.). *Schools and readiness.* Available from http://www.schoolsafety.us/Schools-amp-Readiness-p-11.html (includes links to a lot of great resources about bullying, creating safe schools, and other planning information)

Important Aspects of a School Safety Plan

> Videojug (Interviewer) & Dorn, M. (Interviewee). (n.d.). Developing a school safety plan [Video file]. Available from www.videojug.com/interview/developing-a-school-safety-plan-2 (includes links to a series of school safety videos)

Steps for Creating a Safe Classroom

> No Bully. (2009). *Teachers resources: Follow these steps for creating a safe classroom.* Available from www.nobully.com/teachers.htm

Blue Print for Success for Schools

> Utterly Global. (n.d.). *Best practices: Blue print for success.* Available from http://antibullyingprograms.org/Best_Practice.html

Practical Information on Crisis Planning:
A Guide for Schools and Communities

> Office of Safe and Drug-Free Schools. (2007). *Practical information on crisis planning: A guide for schools and communities.* Available from www.ccsd.k12.co.us/documents/provider/163crisisplanning.pdf

Green Cleaning in Schools Fact Sheet

> Florida Alliance for Healthy Indoor Environments. (n.d.). *Green cleaning in schools* [Fact sheet]. Available from www.childproofing.org/documents/green_cleaning_packet_guidelines_and_definitions.pdf

Children's Environmental Health Network

> Children's Environmental Health Network. (n.d.). *Guiding principles for children and environmental health.* Available from www.cehn.org

Resource Guide

> Children's Environmental Health Network. (2006, July 14). *Resource guide on children's environmental health.* Available from www.cehn.org/cehn/resourceguide/rgtoc.html

EPA Healthy School Environments

> Environmental Protection Agency. (2009, September 24). *Healthy school environments.* Available from www.epa.gov/schools (includes links to healthy environment webcasts and resources)

The Green Schools Alliance

> Global Environmental Options. (2007–2009). Available from www.greenschoolsalliance.org

Sample School Board Resolution

> Green Schools Initiative. (n.d.). *Sample school board resolution: Blueprint for healthy, environmentally sound schools.* Available from http://greenschools.net/article.php?id=192

EPA's Tools for Schools Program

> Environmental Protection Agency. (2010). *IAQ tools for schools program.* Available from www.epa.gov/iaq/schools (a toolkit and resources for schools about how to improve the environmental health of schools)

School Environmental Health and Safety Program

> Washington State Department of Health. (2010). *School environmental health and safety program.* Available from www.doh.wa.gov/ehp/ts/School/ (provides multiple resources on a variety of environmental health issues in schools)

School Environmental Health Resources and Plans

Healthy Schools Campaign. (n.d.). *School environmental health.* Available from www.healthyschoolscampaign.org/programs/envhealth

Support for Breastfeeding in the Workplace

Shealy, K. R., Li, R., Benton-Davis, S., Grummer-Strawn, L. M. (2005). Support for breastfeeding in the workplace. In *The CDC guide to breastfeeding interventions* (pp. 7–12). Available from www.cdc.gov/breastfeeding/pdf/BF_guide_2.pdf (information for employers and working mothers)

Shealy, K. R., Li, R., Benton-Davis, S., Grummer-Strawn, L. M. (2005). *The CDC guide to breastfeeding interventions.* Available from www.cdc.gov/breastfeeding/pdf/breastfeeding_interventions.pdf

CHAPTER THREE

Ever-Higher Expectations

Abby is the kind of teacher who parents dream of their kids having. Enthusiastic, positive, bright, and shiny, she exudes happiness and confidence, as well as the ability to inspire and direct kids with style and grace. Being a music teacher was ingrained in her family, as her parents both taught their entire professional lives. She is tall, commanding attention, but with an open, warm face that sets one completely at ease.

Colleagues would walk by her classroom and see her bouncing around the room, leading students in groups to play handmade instruments, write songs, and sing out. Students were engaged, lively, and creating music—and many times they were style conscious, image unsure, preadolescent fifth and sixth graders.

She was also a dream to work with; constantly teaming with other teachers, respecting valued class time when planning her music lessons, and working to meet the needs of kids. She remained positive, professional, and flexible. The teachers, kids, and principal loved and greatly admired her.

So of course, the staff was shocked when she announced she was quitting teaching and moving on to another field. If you watched her day to day, it became obvious why she was leaving, said one of her colleagues. She was always staying late, e-mailing schedules, seeking out teachers and students to schedule lessons,

(Continued)

(Continued)

and communicating with parents. Hers was not a sustainable model. She said, "While teaching, I was very sad and resentful that I gave so much from 8 to 5 and that I was physically and emotionally exhausted when I got home."

When you watched her, though, it was equally obvious she was born to be a teacher. And we've lost her.

UNREALISTIC EXPECTATIONS

In the last few decades, education has seen a perpetual increase in the expectations of teachers. The list of responsibilities continues to grow exponentially in our standardized-testing environment. Teachers are expected to meet the instructional needs of every child (regardless of how many children are in the room); advocate for special services; make sure that children are fed, clothed, emotionally balanced, healthy, and not bullying others or being abused; communicate frequently with parents; conduct ongoing assessments; complete relicensure paperwork; attend regular workshops and courses; serve on multiple committees and attend meetings; perform clerical and custodial duties; collaborate with staff—and the list goes on and on. And every year, there seem to be a few more items. Many of the expectations are not directly related to teaching students, which is where the motivation of most teachers lies.

This state of affairs is exhausting and dispiriting. Many teachers shared that they simply don't have enough time to do everything they feel they should be doing. And it is eroding their personal and professional lives. In the words of Roland Barth (2004), author of *Learning By Heart*, "Endless uncompensated add-ons eventually lead to the school equivalent of a sweat shop" (p. 90).

THE TIME CRUNCH: DO MORE WITH LESS

Ask teachers what they need more of, and time is usually first on their list. Time for meaningful assessment. Time to collaborate with peers. Time to plan for instruction to help meet the needs of their students.

Teachers are constantly pulled in a million directions, needing to do much more than their schedule and time allow. Day after day, they leave work frustrated that they didn't get more done. And this perpetual feeling of barely keeping your head above water doesn't go away, even for the veteran teachers. It simply becomes the way it is.

One master teacher I interviewed worked just as long and as hard as the new teachers. This was a 30-year veteran. She often wondered out loud why she was still there at 5 p.m. She spent most Saturdays working for hours at school. At her age, shouldn't this have gotten easier by now?

The answer is no. The job keeps getting harder and harder: More standards, mandates, and assessments are imposed by the system. And more students exhibit special education, behavioral, emotional, and social needs. Combine this with the other problems in public education, and it is no wonder teachers are tired, overwhelmed, and frustrated. The author of *Learning By Heart* quotes a teacher speaking about the piling on of duties and obligations for teachers, "When was the last time someone said to me, 'Sandra, you are no longer responsible for . . . '? It's always an add-on" (Barth, 2004, p. 90).

Colleen, who taught in an urban middle school, shared the following:

> My husband was a great moral support, but I couldn't help but hate him and his job as a programmer. He could sleep through his alarm, and it wouldn't be a disaster if he was a half hour late. He could go to the bathroom when he wanted. He could go out to lunch with his colleagues. He worked on his project for eight hours a day, and when it was time, he could come home and didn't have to plan or grade. He didn't deal with constant noise and chaos and power struggles and have people questioning everything he did. He could call in sick without a second thought and not have to worry about sub plans at 3 a.m. when you're puking your guts out.

The frustration in Colleen's comment strikes right at the core of how the cumulative effects of these issues can drive away talented teachers.

Christie is a former high school teacher. She decided not to go back to teaching after spending a few years at home with her kids. At the top of her list was the time problem:

When I taught, I left for work at 5:30 a.m., got home at 4:30 p.m., and spent three to four hours a night (plus a lot of weekend time) planning, grading, etc. Now that I have children, I really wanted a job I could just leave at work, and I don't think teaching is that job. I'm sure some of that would get easier with time; people would always tell me that the first three years are the hardest, but I'm just not up to starting all over.

PROFESSIONAL DEVELOPMENT THAT DOESN'T SPEAK TO REAL CONCERNS

Ask teachers what they want to do during their next inservice day. Most would say grade papers and plan curriculum. Many would say meet with other teachers to collaborate and share curriculum, ideas, and teaching techniques. It's likely that none would say sit through a presentation by someone who hasn't been teaching for over 10 years to learn something they might never use—or discuss philosophy, like mission statements and other topics that don't apply to daily life in a school. Yet that is what most often happens during inservice days.

Teachers are crunched for time to do their jobs well and fully. So taking their time with issues that aren't practical or don't relate to their instruction is disrespectful. Several teachers I interviewed said that when administrators didn't understand or respect the time-management challenges teachers face, they grew increasingly frustrated.

A high school teacher offered the following advice:

Simply: Give teachers time to plan. My greatest pet peeve is administrators who talk merely to hear themselves talk, while a bunch of teachers are forced to sit and watch their workday go by. I think taking up the time that's been designated for planning is a true sign that administrators are out of touch with the realities of the teaching profession or too self-centered to consider the real needs of the people who they depend upon the most.

Every minute of every workday is paramount in a teacher's day. That's why you'll see so many trying to grade or type while eating their lunches. When administrators come and sit down to chat—while it is good for developing a relationship—it is stressful to the teacher who is running around the classroom trying to get ready for the next class. Similarly, it would be helpful if administrators could avoid scheduling a training or philosophical discussion right before the school year begins, when everyone needs to be setting up their rooms. As the teacher quoted above pointed out, this disconnect of the working reality for teachers is frustrating and stressful.

When asked on a *Teacher Magazine* forum (Robora, 2008) what kind of professional development teachers thought "really worked and benefited your instruction and that you would like to see more of," teachers responded that they wanted more time to collaborate, to hear from other teachers, and to learn real, relevant skills that are directly applicable to the classroom. One teacher posted the following message (Dr. Bernard, 2008):

Teachers need the chance to grow through leading other teachers. Teacher leadership is a valuable source of professional development, particularly in these times of diminishing budgets. Teachers can share best practices with other teachers and receive feedback in small group sharing sessions, all while keeping a focus on the goal of increased student achievement.

Another important component is planning time—if a teacher lacks adequate planning time, all the best practices gained in these sharing sessions will remain in a folder on the desk instead of being implemented.

THE THREAT TO HEALTH AND WELL-BEING

Teachers I spoke with shared their personal experiences about how the time-management issue affected their health and their relationships. In this way, this problem couldn't be more personal.

Carol, a 48-year-old veteran teacher at a suburban middle school expressed her concern:

> I am overworked, stressed out, and have gained five to eight pounds a year from overeating, chronic sleep deprivation, and lack of exercise. Over the summer, I realized that this is going to kill me (literally) if I don't figure out how to balance. I am considering taking a leave next year and investigating my options if I can't live in balance and also feel good about the quality of my work.

Here is a teacher who wants to do her best, be the best teacher she can possibly be. But the demands of the job were simply not sustainable for Carol. The lack of balance between her work and personal life left her overweight, sick, and tired. It seems likely that this committed, motivated, and extremely hardworking teacher could be lost to another career, all because of the cumulative effects of teaching on her health.

Effects on health and personal relationships were also on the mind of Chris, a fifth-grade teacher:

> In my current state of mind, sadly, the pleasures associated with having that perfect connection with the students during a great lesson are being overshadowed by the constant mental and physical fatigue resulting from being pulled in ten different directions by all the other duties that come with a day of "teaching." TEACHING seems like it is the last priority most days on the job. Being a secretary, test administrator, test analyzer, and my own advocate for equitable treatment seem to consume what little prep time I have before the school day gets underway. I end up taking correcting and planning home to often work an extra three to five hours into my evening when I should have been spending time with my wife, relaxing, and exercising.

It gets even more personal when relationships are affected by the repeated stress of time management. John, who taught middle school science and math, described how much paperwork he had to do and how this caused stress in his marriage:

Grades were due every nine weeks. I would have papers piled up all over my desk. I had 28 kids in a class, and 10 classes with full, detailed lab reports, portfolio math problems, and other authentic assessments that took over 20 minutes each to grade. I would stay up all night, come home and shower, then go back and teach. It wore on my wife and me, until she finally encouraged me to get out of teaching.

Of course, John's model of teaching was, ultimately, not sustainable for his personal or professional life. Something had to give. As education professionals, we owe it to future teachers to create more opportunities for teachers not only to feel success, collaborate, and do their best work but also to take care of themselves and their families.

Teacher Wellness Activities

- Climate committee that takes turns monthly to plan social activities and bring goodies to staff meetings and the staff room
- Prizes, snacks, raffles, and 50/50 draws at staff meetings
- Snacks at recess
- Wellness bulletin board in staff room
- Inspirational or humorous sayings and jokes around staff room and on wellness board
- Announcements on bathroom walls
- Newspaper articles about teachers' positive impact in mailboxes
- Appreciation assemblies
- Small gifts such as colored pens or greetings in mailboxes
- Share info such as website articles
- Birthday celebrations
- Secret Santa or secret pal at Christmas time
- Monthly socials such as a pool tournament, wine tasting contests, potluck suppers
- Reading club
- Golf tournament
- Car/road rally

(Continued)

(Continued)

- Barbeques
- District wellness cookbook
- Care packages from staff for members who need a "pick me up"
- Humor workshop
- Wellness hikes/walks on a PD day followed by hot chocolate and goodies at the school
- Catered lunch during PD/PT days [Professional Development and Inservice]
- Bowling with prizes
- Volleyball game
- Massages for interested staff members
- Dessert party after school
- Wellness fitness room
- Birthday calendar, cakes once a month for teachers who have their birthdays that month
- Parties to welcome new staff
- Dollar store mugs for teachers' birthdays
- Brown bag lunches at noon hour on staff's hobbies
- Divisional wellness library—books, CDs, DVDs, audio books on an iPod Shuffle for people to borrow

Source: Well Teacher (n.d.).

you can... DO IT! RECOMMENDATIONS FOR ADMINISTRATORS AND TEACHER LEADERS

- Plan inservice days and time with empathy and appreciation for teachers. The more concise, direct, and efficient the meetings are, the more time can be given to teachers to meet, plan, and prepare for students. Encourage staff input on the best use of inservice time.

- On a daily basis, work to support teachers in their quest to manage expectations of the job. Be aware of your impact as you discuss something with a teacher during lunch, right before class, while the teacher is on the way to the bathroom, or as a teacher is leaving for the day. The entire school staff can work on this together.

- Don't simply encourage collaboration; it's not enough. Schedule it during the school day and year. Time should be allotted at least weekly (or at best, daily). Think and schedule creatively so teachers across grade levels and subject areas can observe each other, reflect, and grow as teachers.

- One idea for how to increase the time that teachers can collaborate is to have a weekly or monthly afternoon release time for physical or teamwork activities. One school in my area does this, and students participate in cross-country skiing, hiking, low-ropes courses, and swimming, among other activities that promote healthy lifestyles and fight obesity; while teachers meet, plan, and collaborate.

- Provide support and check-ins for teachers' personal health and well-being, and investigate wellness programs in your area. Some states have wellness programs that motivate participants with giveaways, contests, regular check-ins, and community sports events.

- Implement special activities that show your respect for teachers' time. One idea is a 30-minute respite on a teacher's birthday, which I learned about in *Motivating and Inspiring Teachers* (Whitaker, Whitaker, & Lumpa, 2000). For a simple birthday treat, the administrator gives a teacher a half hour of time. The principal teaches the class for a half hour and gives the teacher a much-needed birthday break. This is a great way to gain insight into the classroom environment while supporting the teacher.

- Utilize support staff to cover duties (while maintaining their lunch break). Teacher time would be better used for planning than supervising noninstructional time.

- U.S. schools have far greater hours of teaching versus higher-performing European and Asian countries, who have far more time for collaborative planning and job-embedded, practical, and relevant professional development, according to *Professional Learning in the Learning Profession: A Status Report on Teacher Development in the United States and Abroad* (Wei, Darling-Hammond,

Andree, Richardson, & Orphanos, 2009). The report makes several recommendations about how the United States can improve student performance by allowing more time for teachers to plan, collaborate, and attend professional development activities within the workday:

1. Professional development should be intensive, ongoing, and connected to practice.

2. Professional development should focus on student learning and address the teaching of specific curriculum content.

3. Professional development should align with school-improvement priorities and goals.

4. Professional development should build strong working relationships among teachers.

 ## WORDS OF WISDOM FROM VETERAN TEACHERS

Veteran teachers recommend setting limits on their workdays. By designating certain hours or a specific amount of time for tasks, they prioritize and are as efficient as possible. They set limits, they say no sometimes, and they speak up about unrealistic expectations. Chris, a fifth-grade teacher, said, "I realized a few years ago that I wouldn't last if I continued working without equitable compensation, so I refused to continue to work for free. 'I finish what I can in a nine-hour workday, and that's all I can do' is my motto now." Many teachers try to strike a balance so they can exercise, spend time with their families, and teach, but it remains a constant challenge.

Along with that, they carry the realization that they will not get everything done, that there is always more to do. But they must take care of themselves. They've learned that taking care of themselves on a daily basis is the only way to ensure mental and physical health. This is much easier said than done, and teachers need support in this from school staff, the community, and administrators to make their model of teaching sustainable.

New York Times education blogger and veteran teacher Stacie Valdez (2006) mentors new teachers. She hosts regular luncheons for mentors and mentees, and she shares her favorite tips:

> For one lunch, I invited other teachers. I asked that each bring an unwritten tip or rule for new teachers as their admittance. Some of the best ones include the following:
>
> - Just say NO!
> - Don't let anyone know you are good at doing something or you'll be doing it for everyone.
> - Reserve one day every weekend to do NO schoolwork—don't even think about school.
> - Exercise.
> - Talk to students in the same manner you want them to talk to you.
> - Be careful what you wish for.
> - Laugh—keep your sense of humor. (para. 10)

Veteran teachers also advocate for planning time during the school day and during inservice times. This way, it is not adding on to the school day or creating more work. They work with administrators to schedule time to meet with grade-level teams, special educators, and other staff to plan curriculum and plan for student needs.

SUCCESS STORIES: PROFESSIONAL LEARNING COMMUNITIES AND COLLABORATION TIME

Professional learning communities take off. In the book *Professional Learning Communities at Work,* by DuFour and Eaker (1998), one of the essential characteristics of professional learning communities (PLCs) is for teachers to work in collaborative teams to learn, experiment, and grow. The book goes on to describe a scenario of a first-year teacher who is hired into a PLC (defined as "teams of educators systematically working together to improve teaching practice and student learning," Starr, 2006, para. 1). It is clear that the school in the scenario valued peer collaboration and professional development and set aside time for teachers to do it. According to the scenario, "In addition to the teacher planning days at the start of the year, the five half-days and three full days set aside for professional development, and the common preparation periods allocated for teaching teams, teachers were given two hours every two weeks for planning and conferencing" (DuFour & Eaker, 1998, p. 41).

In fact, most of the teacher literature explains how teachers should have built-in time to meet with grade-level peers, both in their own schools and across the district, and for new teachers to be mentored by experienced teachers for several years. This all takes time, and there is already not enough of it. So much of the time for planning and collaborating doesn't happen, or doesn't happen fully. And it would make everyone better teachers. Fortunately, the implementation of PLCs, and of job-embedded professional development models in general, is a growing phenomenon.

Sherman Oaks provides built-in collaboration time for teachers. Not all schools are accepting the model of increasing expectations for teachers while not providing adequate built-in hours for planning, collaboration, and professional development. At Sherman Oaks Community Charter School in California, teachers have 90 uninterrupted minutes daily to meet, collaborate, plan, and problem solve (Curtis, 2000).

In an era of dwindling budgets and jam-packed agendas, this may seem impossible. Not so, says Principal Peggy Bryan (Curtis, 2000). At Sherman Oaks, "Teachers meet while students have lunch, study hall, and a recreation period. Paraprofessionals—usually parents—come in during that time and oversee the children. 'It's simple, inexpensive, and it makes all the difference'" (para. 8), she said.

While the format is always under revision, teachers use this time for planning, grade-level meetings, cross-grade meetings, and problem solving. This lends itself to a feeling of professionalism, colleagueship, and support. "It's always wonderful stuff—things that get your brain stretched," says teacher Barbara Lynn (Curtis, 2000) of the content of the midday block. "I feel like a professional" (para. 3). By providing built-in opportunities like this, Sherman Oaks fosters a collaborative community that works together to support every child, and every teacher as they constantly hone and learn their craft.

The 90-minute collaborative block is not all that Sherman Oaks does to promote professional development. They also employ a full-time substitute teacher. This allows Sherman Oaks educators to travel to professional development opportunities that teachers deem valuable. The one requirement is that teachers come back and share their knowledge, often during the daily 90-minute blocks. This way, the professional development each teacher completes impacts the entire staff, elevating everyone.

By creative planning, and a collaborative approach to leadership, school leaders can stop the rush-rush mentality and lack of planning time that drive teachers from the classroom. Sherman Oaks is a model for how schools can use their greatest assets to better serve students, school staff, and morale (Curtis, 2000).

 ## THE SILVER LINING: CHALLENGING AND ALWAYS CHANGING

One thing teachers will tell you is that they are rarely bored on any given teaching day. Seldom a day goes by in the classroom where everything goes as expected. Discussions often end up in places you would never imagine. Even when teaching the same subject matter, teachers find that students, with all their intricacies and complexities, change the course and dialogue of a day in innumerable ways.

In many cases, teachers are not the type of people you would find behind a desk all day. They are a blur of constant motion, feet jiggling, and palpable energy. The job keeps them engaged, on their feet, and making countless small and large decisions on any given day.

Depending on the school and situation, teaching can also foster an expression of creativity and autonomy that motivates teachers. "One very positive thing about the school where I teach and my subject (English) is that I have a great deal of autonomy and can be creative. I can basically choose what texts I want to teach and, for the most part, how I want to teach them, and this gives me great satisfaction," said high school teacher Jeff.

This autonomy and decision-making power afforded to some teachers also results in less teacher attrition, according to Borman and Dowling (2008), in *Review of Educational Research*. So the positive aspects about Jeff's English teaching position will also serve to sustain him in this ever-changing field. Having a school that believes in its teachers' ability to design creative curriculum and that provides the support to implement and make important decisions about it empowers teachers. By creating a culture where creative and innovative teachers are supported, teachers rise to the occasion.

Sonia Nieto's (2005) book *Why We Teach* features 21 educators answering the complex question of why they teach. The idea of her work being a constant process of learning, for both herself and her students, motivates teacher Jennifer Welborn:

> I love being on the move, being flexible, negotiating, multitasking, helping, listening, creating, laughing, and loving. I am passionate about being with kids, helping them learn or unlearn things, and perhaps changing their lives in subtle and not-so-subtle ways. Being with young people, particularly young adolescents, suits my personality. They are fun, refreshingly honest and open. They are sincere and unpredictable. They are always forgiving. (p. 16)

Jennifer astutely describes how teaching is not for the faint of heart or the person seeking predictability. Every day is different, every year a new chance, every child unique and brilliant in different and changing ways.

A librarian values the creativity and opportunities for professional development that teaching offers:

> I love my work because I can constantly craft what I do, taking advantage of new learning and inspirations from many sources. I can't think of any other profession where one can be so creative within the guidelines for the job. There's always a new opportunity to try something out, as well as many chances to hone an idea to keep making that idea get better and better. There is always a new class of kids who will respond differently to what we do, and the challenge of reaching each kid is exhilarating. We are more supported, as well as required, to keep taking courses and improving ourselves much more regularly than in any other profession.

Most teachers are lifelong learners and want to continually improve their craft. If given access to professional development during their paid work time, most—if not all—teachers will happily attend meaningful training to improve their work with students.

Despite increasing expectations, many teachers thrive on the constantly changing, always challenging, and ever-evolving field of education.

ADDITIONAL RESOURCES

Print Resources

Graves, D. (2001). *The energy to teach.* Portsmouth, NH: Heinemann.

Kottler, E., Kottler, J., & Kottler, C. (2003). *Secrets for secondary school teachers: How to succeed in your first year* (2nd ed.). Thousand Oaks, CA: Corwin.

Luckner, J., & Rudolph, S. (2009). *Teach well, live well strategies for success.* Thousand Oaks, CA: Corwin.

Schwartz, N. (2008). *The teacher chronicles: Confronting the demands of students, parents, administrators, and society.* New York: Laurelton Media.

Thompson, J. (2007). *First-year teachers' survival guide: Ready-to-use strategies, tools, & activities for meeting the challenges of each school day.* San Francisco: Jossey-Bass.

Valentine, S. (2009). *Everything but teaching: Planning, paperwork, and processing.* Thousand Oaks, CA: Corwin.

Vandenberghe, R., & Huberman, A. M. (1999). *Understanding and preventing teacher burnout.* Boston: Cambridge University Press.

Whitaker, T. (2003). *What great teachers do differently: Fourteen things that matter most.* Larchmont, NY: Eye on Education.

Yendol-Hoppey, D., & Dana, N. (2010). *Powerful professional development: Building expertise within the four walls of your school.* Thousand Oaks, CA: Corwin.

Internet Resources

Stress Management for Teachers and Students

Education World. (2005). *How do you spell "stress relief"?* Available from www.educationworld.com/a_issues/issues/issues181.shtml

Education World. (2009). *From chaos to coherence: Managing teacher stress.* Available from www.education-world.com/a_admin/admin/admin413.shtml

National Education Association. (n.d.). *Stress management for teachers and students.* Available from www.nea.org/tools/30319.htm

Time-Management Tips for Teachers

Wagner, K. J. (2004). *Time saving tips for teachers.* Available from www.educationoasis.com/resources/Articles/time_saving_tips.htm

Keeping Teachers Healthy: A Successful School Wellness Program

Allen, R. (2004, Winter). Keeping teachers healthy: Staff wellness program yields results. *Curriculum Update.* Available from www.ascd.org/publications/curriculum_update/winter2004/Keeping_Teachers_Healthy.aspx

Bureaucracy

Sarah scrambles around the school during her only prep period, avoiding the stack of papers to grade and e-mails to return. She is a blur of motion, filling out the appropriate forms for field-trip approval; checking calendars, schedules, and available funds; calling the destination; and organizing buses and bag lunches for the trip. Sarah knows she won't finish all of this work during her 40-minute block, but she will work at a frantic pace, to complete as much as possible. Every minute this takes, she knows, will increase the work she must do at home to stay on top of her planning and curriculum. But she tells herself repeatedly that it is worth it: Her students will benefit. A nagging voice tells her it's easier to not plan these trips, to stay at school and have her prep time, lunches, and supervision already planned out. Sarah quells the thought and continues, barely stopping to use the bathroom before her students return. Now, she's back to teaching for the rest of the day.

Several days pass, with Sarah working at every available time when students are not in the room (which is not much of the day!) to coordinate this trip to a low-ropes course, where her students will develop the much-needed skills of teamwork and problem solving. She writes the permission slips, adds the health forms, and calls and organizes parent chaperones. Now, she is really behind in her grading and planning and knows she faces a weekend of catching up.

(Continued)

(Continued)

During her lunch, Sarah eats and grades at the same time. When she is behind, she typically eats at her desk, using every available minute she can. The phone rings. It's a parent asking what the field trip has to do with academics, proclaiming that it is not real learning and therefore his child will not attend: They will do something educational. The parent continues, "And I am not the only parent who feels this way. I've talked to several others who feel this field trip will have no benefit toward the academic success of their children. I wouldn't be surprised if you get a call from other parents about this."

Sarah gulps for air, her face reddening. She thanks the parent for his feedback, stares at her half-eaten lunch and stack of papers, and begins to cry. She mumbles, "It's just not worth it," to an empty classroom.

The way schools function and are led can cause unintended consequences for teachers and students. Multiple layers of bureaucracy with tasks, such as setting up field trips, acquiring supplies, and following chopped-up schedules, can frustrate and alienate teachers, driving them away from the kind of teaching they want to do and know is best for their students. In many cases, teachers carry all the responsibility but none of the decision-making power—for curricular decisions, assessment tools, or schedules—for choices that they must adhere to and are judged by, even when they are not what the educator thinks is best.

FIELD TRIPS: NO GOOD DEED GOES UNPUNISHED

Some of us go into teaching with naïve grand visions of unconventional, integrated teaching with wide swaths of time at our disposal, the materials that we need, and the academic freedom to explore children's innate interests and abilities. Sadly, teachers soon learn that this kind of teaching and learning is not realistic, and is often not supported by budgets, administrators, or educational leaders.

Take for example a simple field trip, as illustrated in the vignette above. The teacher will dedicate hours, if not days, to this multistep journey (more time than already limited prep time allows): Taking into account dwindling school budgets, the teacher will calculate the cost of the trip—and determine whether funds are available. Next, the teacher will schedule the field trip with the destination and, perhaps, make a site visit. These steps can take days, with rescheduling and multiple call backs. After that comes the creation of a permission slip detailing the information. Finally, the teacher will find responsible parent chaperones; organize the children into groups (keeping delicate behavior issues in mind); assign leaders to each group; contact the nurse; coordinate special needs; and troubleshoot. This is before they even walk out the door.

On the day of the trip, the teacher is responsible for students having what they need, their general safety, and their behavior on the bus. Teachers use their normal prep periods for field trips; spending the day organizing, leading, and guiding students. Field trips require extra prep time—more prep time than allotted—time meant for curricular planning, grading, communicating with parents, and unexpected needs that arise. Teachers are forced to choose between planning time and hands-on teaching (two critical aspects of the teaching profession).

One teacher of fifth-grade students describes the field-trip experience:

On field-trip days I come to school early, to gather first-aid supplies and parent permission slips. Then, I organize my children to board the school bus, manage their behavior on a loud, uncomfortable ride, and then manage their behavior during a performance. During this time, I am missing my precious preparation periods, in which I need to plan for my afternoon classes. We leave at 8 a.m. and return at noon. No one else is in my classroom, and I haven't been able to use a bathroom all morning. My only time to eat, use the bathroom, make a parent phone call, and prep for my afternoon classes is the 20 minutes I have when my students are at lunch from 1:10 to 1:30. Something is really wrong here.

Every new teacher dreams of taking students on field trips and overnights. But the reality is much different from the dream.

In many cases, the teacher is solely responsible to make these events happen, and the workload increases exponentially because of it—not to mention the increased liability and the overtime hours required by an overnight trip.

It's no wonder that some teachers stop planning and doing field trips altogether.

COMMITTEES:
THE DEATH OF CREATIVE IDEAS

When a teacher has an idea for a schoolwide event, there is lots of preparation and planning involved to make it happen. New teachers (and experienced, innovative teachers) come with new ideas for schoolwide or grade-level activities to generate excitement and enthusiasm about learning. Often, they are greeted with less-than-enthusiastic staff members who are too busy to want to give time and energy to a new and different event or activity. They are not to blame, necessarily, because they have probably seen too many events that are disorganized, time consuming, or where the final planning and responsibility ends up with the teacher.

In *Educating Esmé* (Codell, 2001), the author describes her experience, as a new teacher, of presenting her first creative idea for a schoolwide Fairy Tale Festival:

> Mr. Turner [her principal] approved it, but he said that the idea has to first go through administrators, teachers, and community members. I showed my idea to the librarian-to-be. She was skeptical. . . . Sometimes I think, Why invent projects? What is the point? How will I ever accomplish what I set out to do, what I imagine? Then I think of the past, even before I was born, the great small feats people accomplished. I think of things like Mary Martin washing her hair onstage in *South Pacific*, or the Kungsholm puppet operas with sixty puppets on stage at once, or the palace built by the postman in France, or the circus I saw in Copenhagen where a woman wore a coat of live minks, or any of the things I enjoy and value, and I think: Those people had to work to accomplish those things, they thought of details, they followed through. Even if I come off as naïve and zealous, even if I get on everyone's nerves, I have to

follow these examples. Even if I fail, I have to try and try and try. It may be exhausting, but that is beside the point. The goal is not necessarily to succeed but to keep trying, to be the kind of person who has ideas and sees them through. (From *Educating Esmé*, by Esmé Raji Codell, ©2001 by Esmé Raji Codell. Reprinted by permission of Algonquin Books of Chapel Hill. All rights reserved, p. 7)

Esmé was endlessly frustrated by the critical, skeptical staff in her school. She goes on to describe what happened to her Fairy Tale Festival proposal:

Perhaps I will look back on this and think, as I was most condescendingly informed yesterday at the Friends of the School Library Committee meeting (which I organized, by the way, after it was explained to me that a committee needed to be invented because a committee needs to exist to approve a proposal), that it was not realistic to do, as I would surely have known had I been teaching awhile. I said everything I proposed I would be willing to coordinate, that I just needed help on the actual day of the festival to supervise for the children's safety. The vice principal, Ms. Coil, said no, everything should be a group effort. Then, as a group, they decided they didn't want to put forth the effort. (From *Educating Esmé*, by Esmé Raji Codell, ©2001 by Esmé Raji Codell. Reprinted by permission of Algonquin Books of Chapel Hill. All rights reserved, p. 9)

Esmé's struggles clearly show how the educational system can stifle creativity and ideas from new and experienced teachers. Her story demonstrates how committees can operate in reverse of how they were intended and serve to complicate matters more than to assist. Esmé was a driven, motivated teacher, who kept on teaching despite this and other challenges thrown her way. Not all teachers have that level of resilience and tolerance. When she is questioning, "Why invent projects? What is the point?" Esmé echoes teachers everywhere who face daunting challenges—in their already busy days—to create rich, diverse and integrated learning experiences for their students. Too many of these creative teachers simply quit, finding a better, higher-paying job that values creative and innovative thinking more than teaching does.

And that is the opposite of what we need in schools. We need these minds who think outside the box to help us face the increasing challenges that make up education in America today.

PURCHASE ORDERS AND CLOSED BUDGETS

Every spring, Michelle embarks on an ambitious educational project and process. She designs, leads, and organizes a service-learning project driven by the interests of her fifth- and sixth-grade students. Among other projects, her students have researched, organized, and set up schoolwide recycling and composting programs; designed and created signs for a nature trail and wetland area; set aside and signed a woodchuck habitat; created an anti-litter educational program and signage; and designed and planted edible and native gardens.

And every spring as she does this, the budget for the school is closed. This means even if she has money in her class funds, she can't use them; any materials (wood for signs, recycling bins, or shovels) have to be borrowed or bought with her own money. Sometimes she has received funds from a community organization.

Now that the economy is tanking, she can't count on any grant money, and her own funds are dwindling. How will she lead this kind of hands-on, inquiry-based project if she has no funds and no support to do so?

The same holds true for any subject and any materials needed for your students. Budgets close for schools between January and March. So if you realize your students have an interest in a topic, and you want to buy books to support that, you are out of luck—unless you appeal to the principal (and then you have to go through paperwork, which can take weeks to complete).

One teacher I interviewed was told that the office staff was hiding the purchase orders from the teachers. They didn't want to process any more purchase orders, or the principal gave them that directive. How does this support creative teaching that is constantly changing, as are the needs of the students?

Teachers often make big school-supply orders in the spring or early summer. The contents are typical: pens, pencils, paper, and erasers. This is supposed to be the bulk of the teachers' purchases for the school year. (In some districts, such basic supplies are not even covered by the budget and teachers end up purchasing them with their own funds; see Chapter 5.)

What is unknown at that point is the developmental level and the needs of the upcoming class, which can be known only after a few weeks or months in the classroom. Then, the teacher will know students' reading levels and abilities and can plan for additional purchases as needed for curricular materials. And this should continue through the year, as the teacher learns more about the students and can find materials to support them, or needs to plan for a new student who moves into the class. Sometimes this doesn't happen. Teachers are left to use what they have, often old and outdated material that might not hold the interest of the students, contributing to increased behavior and motivation problems.

If teachers aren't given the opportunity to use their skills to find, change, or create materials to meet the needs of their students, they will begin to lose the passion and motivation that drove them to teach in the first place.

SCHEDULING: NOT IDEAL FOR STUDENTS OR TEACHERS

The scheduling of instructional and collaborative time is a pressing issue for teachers. Standardized testing and preparation, scripted programs, chopped-up schedules, special education services, and regular interruptions day after day lessen the time available for teachers to engage in innovative lesson planning or creative teaching.

When teachers don't have a say in how their instructional time is broken up, the curriculum they are supposed to teach, or the way that student behavior will be managed, they can grow disenfranchised. Susan Moore Johnson and the Project on the Next Generation of Teachers (2006), "a multi-year, multi-study research project" (p. 13), reported on problems with scheduling collaboration time:

> How their time was scheduled was very important to the new teachers, particularly whether their preparation periods— usually one per day—were coordinated with those of other

teachers who taught the same subject or students. New teachers praised schools that deliberately arranged their schedules so that they could plan classes or review students' progress together. Secondary schools that featured project-based learning, interdisciplinary classes, or team-based instruction often arranged time for teachers to collaborate. But in more traditional secondary schools, preparation periods often seemed haphazardly assigned, more likely the byproduct of a computerized scheduling program than the result of deliberate planning. (p. 18)

Teachers feel that their creativity, exploration, and time have been "hijacked." Here, one teacher responds to an article published by the National Education Association, "Why They Leave" (Kopkowski, 2008):

Over my career, I have experienced many of the scenarios depicted in your article. Yet, somehow I had the "juice" to ride over those hurdles in the past, because I believed in what was happening once I was able to close the door and teach my classes. That is no longer the case, because the heart of our teaching has been hijacked by the standardized tests, the increasingly impossible standard of achievement that is required of our students, and our administrators' fear in response to this. Gone are the moments when we can pursue an idea down a new road for a week or two, or sit for an hour and talk about a social issue that has arisen in our classroom. Each moment is strung with expectations that are directly connected to the curriculum—which, by the way, has been totally rewritten to align directly with the Mastery Tests. (para. 3)

Teachers are often handed schedules to use at the beginning of the year without much say about it. Then, they plan their instructional time around what they are given. This usually means stunted little chunks of time that don't allow for meaningful, in-depth learning to occur. Take a 15-minute time period between a special class and lunch. By the time students transition and are ready for learning, about 10 minutes are left. This is barely enough time to fit in a short read aloud, or play an educational game. Teachers end up feeling like shepherds guiding students to the next activity, instead of providing them with real moments of rich learning.

Here is what one elementary school teacher had to say about scheduling:

> Teachers just work with the schedules they are given. This can mean short time periods where it is hard to get into any real learning. And the priority seems to be the specials classes, and their scheduling issues, not what would be best for our students and their learning. It seems like classroom and curricular needs are last on the totem pool in schedule decisions, when they should be first. Teachers need to have more input on these issues, yet we are too busy teaching to have the time to give it.

The issues around scheduling circle back to previous chapters, detailing the limitations and stressors that standardized testing and increasing expectations place on the daily lives of everyone in the school community.

POLICY: LACK OF INPUT

Ask teachers how they feel about their math program, their reading curriculum, or the assessment system their school uses to communicate with parents, and you will likely get an earful. The trouble is, not many people are asking. According to an article on Teachersnetwork.org (Kumar, 2000), "In education, policies are usually made by school board members and administrators, but teachers are rarely part of the process" (para. 1):

> "Only 39 percent of teachers believed that they had significant influence over discipline policy, content of in-service training (33 percent), grouping of students (29 percent), or establishing curriculum (37 percent)," according to the National Center for Educational Statistics (in Nelson 1994, 88). Unfortunately, a survey of teachers, students, and parents revealed that the 12 areas of inquiry such as instructional programs, supervision of students, student and teacher support, and student safety fell far short of including the opinions of professional staff members on policy matters (School Board of Broward County, 1999, para. 2)

Figure 4.1   Reasons for teacher dissatisfaction (1994–1995)

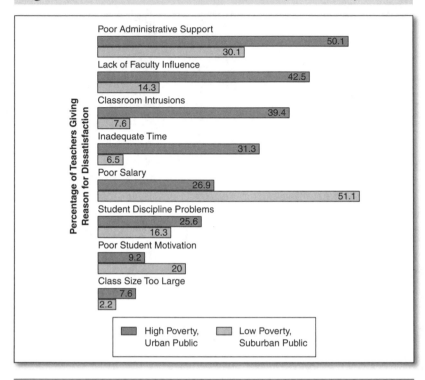

Source: Richard M. Ingersoll, adapted for NCTAF from "Teacher Turnover and Teacher Shortages: An Organizational Analysis." *American Educational Research Journal, 38*(Fall 2001): 499–534.

According to NCTAF (National Commission on Teaching and America's Future, n.d.), "lack of faculty influence" was the third highest reason teachers left the profession (see Figure 4.1). Teachers have the real-life skills to make decisions in the best interests of the education of students, and yet they rarely have an opportunity to make them.

One interviewee described frustration with the school's literacy program:

In the public elementary school I taught in, children choral read stories (BORING stories, too!), the teacher had a script to follow, and there was a day-to-day pacing guide that was followed to the letter. The principal would make rounds to make sure that everyone was on Page 65 of the guide and that they transitioned from language arts time to math time at exactly 10:00. Sure, there are probably some teachers who need their hand held, but the majority of teachers are smart, creative people who can gauge if their class needs to spend 15 more minutes on math today, and can come up with creative ways to get students to learn. The creative, smart ones get frustrated and leave, leaving behind the mediocre teachers who would be fine with just following the pacing guide.

There are numerous ways teachers can get involved in leadership and policy issues, if school districts and administrators give them the professional pay and support to do so. See the recommendations for teacher leaders and administrators section for ideas about how to do this.

RECOMMENDATIONS FOR ADMINISTRATORS AND TEACHER LEADERS

• Work with the school board, the district office, and the superintendent to make sure the budget timing respects education. Student needs and interests don't follow budget timelines. Find ways to fund your teachers' reasonable requests for materials throughout the year, especially for innovative and creative projects.

• Explore ways to assist teachers in field-trip and innovative activity planning. This can include recruiting support from administrators or assigning clerical tasks to administrative support staff or parent volunteers.

• Teachers are anxious for a number of reasons about taking their students on an overnight trip. To make this more manageable, a team could be created of teachers, parents, and administrators to lighten this load. The team would share the full responsibility for the trip, including the supervision during the trip and organizational details.

• Give your teachers the professional respect to deviate from scripted programs as the need arises. Every child is different, every year is different, and therefore, the teaching each year will be different.

• During a series of staff meetings, or with teacher representatives from each grade level, plan a schedule that contains long periods of uninterrupted educational time and that allows for team teaching, subject integration, and in-depth learning whenever possible.

- Teachers can plan interdisciplinary units with students. These would not follow the traditional schedule of classes but would provide opportunities for teams of teachers from across disciplines to work together, while students are able to explore a subject without time-period and subject limitations. This may also free some staff for focused collaboration, planning time, or professional development, because fewer teachers might be needed in different educational settings that integrated learning provides. For example, if a team of middle school students is working on an animal ethics writing piece incorporating science and language arts; the social studies and math teachers might be able to complete some collaboration or planning when they wouldn't have had the opportunity otherwise.

- Work with your district to provide professionally paid and supported leadership and feedback opportunities for teachers in all areas, such as scheduling, program selection, discipline and schoolwide policies, and other schoolwide issues. Following is a list of ways to promote this involvement and teacher leadership, which will increase teacher retention and investment (Johnson & Project on the Next Generation of Teachers, 2006). These are potential areas for teacher leadership with ideas from David Kumar's (2000) article, "Opportunities for Teachers as Policy Makers" (with my discussion of each idea):

1. *Curriculum Planning and Implementation.* Since teachers are doing the actual implementation of programs and curriculum, it makes sense for them to be at the table when decisions about these issues are made. That way, they will be more invested and better able to have success with changes. Too often, politicians or educational experts without much real-life teaching experience make these decisions and wonder why they aren't more successful.

2. *School-Based Management.* This is a use of various school-based leadership programs that incorporate direction and feedback from teachers, administrators, and community members. As Kumar (2000) writes, "As teacher input and

thought in policy decisions are welcomed and valued, teachers become active participants in processes that govern their practices. Understandably, teachers show more commitment and liberty to implement policies they help to develop" (para. 8).

3. *Internal Evaluation.* This refers to teachers taking on various roles in action research, with the goal of evaluating a certain aspect of school functioning. This can only be done professionally with adequate release time and administrative support. Internal evaluation is done in collaboration with school boards, and the teachers are valued as equal partners in problem solving and evaluation.

4. *Technology.* The use of technology has increased the opportunities for teachers to collaborate, communicate, problem solve, and share resources through websites, blogs, forums, and social media. In this way, teachers are also able to influence public policy, by writing about their experiences, and communicating with policy makers.

5. *School Advisory Councils.* This is a collaborative leadership model created by the Florida Department of Education, where parents, teachers, administrators, and community members work together to make school policy decisions. This model of shared leadership is worthy of extensive research as a possible school leadership reform effort.

WORDS OF WISDOM FROM VETERAN TEACHERS

Teachers swim their hardest to stay afloat in the sea of bureaucracy, but they can't do it alone. Anne, an elementary school teacher with 11 years of experience, advises evaluating day-to-day practices:

It's easy to get tunnel vision while teaching, and get stuck in the day-to-day of gritty learning and lessons. From time to time, teachers need to pull their heads up and look around. Is this schedule what is best for students and their learning? Can I participate in planning team teaching and collaboration time? Is there any way to get stronger administrative support for innovative programs? We are all strapped for time, but change only happens when we demand it. After all, teachers know the most about the education of their students. Of course, this needs to be done in a supportive and open environment led by the administration or school leadership team.

Experienced teachers remember that schools were designed to educate students, not to make it easier for the office staff to manage purchase orders and for administrators to close the budget. They advocate for what they need, even when it can be time consuming and challenging.

To plan meaningful field trips, teachers divide and conquer, working as a team to take on all the tasks that this involves. By sharing the responsibility, teachers do not get as overwhelmed. At times, parent volunteers can help with some of this work, as can other teaching and school staff. Some schools even have administrative staff to support organizing field trips, and this would be welcome help at any school.

Some teachers, who are mandated to follow a scripted program, close their classroom doors and deviate from the program as dictated by student need. To them, not to do so would be irresponsible or disrespectful to the students. These teachers use the programs as a base to work from, and they give themselves more freedom than the program allows. This is isolating and, certainly, not a long-term solution. For some teachers, though, it is the only way they can be creative and innovative with their students.

SUCCESS STORIES: REAL-LIFE INTEGRATED LEARNING

When Emily was asked by her principal if she wanted to partner with a local nonprofit and the district support staff to try service learning with her students, she had no idea what she was getting into. As a former environmental educator, she enjoyed doing hands-on science activities with her students, but she had never done service learning with her students before.

She had a lot to learn. Thankfully, Emily's school provided a professional development opportunity to begin to learn about the process of service learning (an instructional approach where students define a problem in their community and then design a way to solve it or improve the situation). Next, Emily partnered with a service-learning expert, who had lots of knowledge of the community, for an independent study of service- and place-based learning. While earning three credits, she and her mentor, along with a community volunteer, planned for meaningful service-learning projects to be completed with her 55 sixth-grade science students. The team met usually during school hours, and Emily's principal provided coverage of some of her duties to do this, so she could keep up with her other school responsibilities such as grading and communicating with parents. This way, Emily was never completely overwhelmed. The service-learning team shared responsibilities, for arranging field trips into the community, for creating the portfolio for students to complete, and for facilitating the groups of students during the project. When problems came up, the team discussed them and decided how to respond. The culminating event was a service-learning fair where the students presented their work to the school community. This event was organized and run by the team, and local media was called to cover the event. Emily's principal helped by supplying the budget for the necessary materials for each project and by creatively scheduling services, specials, and classes around this unique month-long learning experience. The principal also came to the service-learning fair and encouraged all the classes to come as well.

None of this is measured by a standardized test. But if you ask a sixth grader what they did for the service-learning project, you might hear, "I started a recycling program at our school," or "I preserved amphibian habitat on our school campus," or "I wrote and performed a play about the history of our town." Real-life experience, solving real-life problems: That is what service learning is all about. This type of innovative, creative project can only take place when teachers are supported by their principals, fellow teachers, and community members. Together, they can share not only the responsibilities but also ways to manage the complex systemic challenges teachers face.

THE SILVER LINING: MAKING A DIFFERENCE

Even when teachers feel that their voice and leadership may not be valued by politicians and district leaders, they find great satisfaction in their ability to promote social ideals and values such as global citizenship in their students. Teachers want to develop personal relationships, to help their students achieve academically, and to feel as though they are contributing to creating a better society and world. This is another enduring reason why teachers continue to teach.

One anonymous teacher commented that he "wanted to help teach people and make the world a better place. Education can change the world from the foundations. I keep teaching since I feel like I am really making a difference." Changing the world from its foundations. That is a powerful idea, and it motivates teachers.

Take the idea of promoting an environmental ethic. If this is not taught at home, it is teachers who will instill a value of wild places and a responsibility for improving the planet. By recycling, composting, and taking care of their school campus, students develop an environmental awareness they will take into their future jobs and households.

Or maybe it comes in the form of recognizing media pressures or having empathy for people with cultural or religious differences from themselves. These progressive human values will be carried into students' future lives, the imprint of their education perhaps hidden from plain view—certainly not measured on high-stakes tests—but present in the individuals they become.

For Shelley, a reading specialist, the value of becoming a literate and critical-thinking citizen is of utmost importance:

> I teach literacy because my own literacy is my most stalwart companion, and reading and writing have saved my life many times, in one way or another. I want all children to have these skills, and particularly the kids I serve: Many of them do not come from families with a lot of access to institutional power. I want them to grow up with the skills to access that power if they choose to, rather than being shut out from it and stuck in poverty.

As a school nurse explains, the ability to shape the next generation is a motivating factor:

My political views of the world permeate every aspect of my life. I try to live according to my values in everything I do—whether it is recycling my household trash or giving money to eliminate land mines in Afghanistan. I love the concept "Think globally, Act locally." I believe that, although we all need to be thinking of the big picture, change happens on a local level.

Working with children in education is where I believe real change happens. Schools not only teach the scholastic skills that kids need to succeed but—as important—teach them how to be emotionally and physically healthy people who care about others as well as themselves. We are helping the next generation develop their values, beliefs, and relationships with others—and they, in turn, impact their families and friends. Working in education is the best way I know to affect real social and political change. And I see it every day when a student exhibits empathy, compassion, and generosity toward others in the school community.

I will always carry a few memories with me from my elementary schooling: One was watching the movie *Roots* and discussing it with my sixth-grade class. A whole new world of injustice and empathy rose up before me for the first time: These—an awareness of wrong and the capacity for understanding—were embedded in my person. I have never lost the memory; it changed who I was, and who I was to become.

There are essential values that teachers hope to instill in students, to improve our society "from the foundations." Again, it isn't tangible, but for many teachers it is motivating and meaningful. Despite the bureaucracy, teachers work to make positive impacts on future generations every day.

ADDITIONAL RESOURCES

Print Resources

Meier, D. (2002). *In schools we trust.* Boston: Beacon Press.

Nehring, J. (1998). *The school within us: The creation of an innovative public school* (SUNY Series, Democracy and Education). Albany, NY: State University of New York Press.

Spring, S. (2005). *The organized teacher: A hands-on guide to setting up and running a terrific classroom.* New York: McGraw-Hill.

Thurston, C. (2009). *Survival tips for new teachers: From people who have been there (and lived to tell about it).* Fort Collins, CO: Cottonwood Press.

Valentine, S. (2009). *Everything but teaching: Planning, paperwork, and processing.* Thousand Oaks, CA: Corwin.

Internet Resources

Bending Bureaucracy to Kids' Needs

Friedman, R. (2008, June 10). *Bending bureaucracy to kids' needs in Great Neck.* Available from www.publicschoolinsights.org/node/2027

Bureaucracy and Public Education Statistics

Common Good. (n.d.). *Law and public education: The paralyzing effects of excessive bureaucracy* [Fact sheet]. Available from http://commongood.org/learn-reading-cgpubs-factsheets-7.html

The Importance of Creativity and Innovation in Schools

Davies, T. (2000, Fall). Confidence! Its role in the creative teaching and learning of design and technology. *Journal of Technology Education.* Available from http://scholar.lib.vt.edu/ejournals/JTE/v12n1/pdf/davies.pdf

Chapter Five

Respect and Compensation

Stephanie, a single mom, sat in her small apartment staring at the application for food stamps in disbelief. This was not how she had pictured her life. When she went into teaching, she knew she wouldn't be making tons of money. But she didn't think she would end up barely making ends meet, struggling to pay her grocery bills, medical expenses, and rent. She had her master's in music education, after all, and was a professional educator. But it didn't matter. Her job at the school barely paid $800 dollars every two weeks. In addition to her job teaching elementary school music, she gave individual lessons and worked as a community and school coordinator. Her three different jobs in total amounted to well over a full-time work week.

What bothered Stephanie more than anything, however, was the possible effect that her financial troubles might have on her little girl. Stephanie's daughter has autism, and she spends countless hours navigating how to get her the services she needs: time when she should be sleeping, or taking care of herself.

Now she sits with the food-stamp application, fills it out, and sighs. She is still not sure exactly how she ended up in this situation. Stephanie was taught if you work hard, and make good decisions, you will be a success. In her experience, this is far from reality.

STRUGGLING TO MAKE ENDS MEET

Stephanie is a real teacher struggling to make ends meet in America, and she is not alone. Many of the respondents to my surveys talked about how they struggle with the low salaries teachers make when compared to similarly trained professionals in other fields (see Figure 5.1).

One teacher (whose grade level and school type were undisclosed) felt this disappointment, also:

> Pay was very frustrating, too. If I hadn't been married, I wouldn't have been able to afford to live in the county in which I taught. Almost every other teacher in our school had a second job as a waitress, a bartender, a retail clerk. I looked on a salary scale website, and it was pretty discouraging to see that I could make more as an entry-level secretary or housepainter with a high school diploma than I was making with a college degree and master's credits. I might have been able to tolerate the stress and physical strain if I had been well compensated, but $30,000 a year to take emotional abuse every day of your life: not cool.

Teachers begin their careers feeling disrespected, because their salaries are so incommensurate with what other professionals earn. New teachers in America can expect to earn about $34,935 a year, according to a recent study by the National Educational Association (NEA, 2009b). When you compare that with $42,123 for beginning management trainees, $47,453 for beginning public accounting professionals, and $51,341 for beginning registered nurses, it looks particularly bleak (NEA, 2009b).

The situation doesn't seem to be improving. "Teacher salaries have risen a scant 0.8 percent since 1996, says the Economic Policy Institute. That's a whole lot less than the 12 percent increase other college-educated workers have enjoyed over the same period" (Flannery, 2007, para. 4). In many districts, teacher pay is actually going down, when you consider that the contributions to health care have gone up significantly (Allegretto, Corcoran, & Mishel, 2008). And teachers are fighting threats of

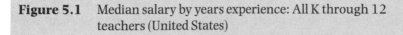

Figure 5.1   Median salary by years experience: All K through 12 teachers (United States)

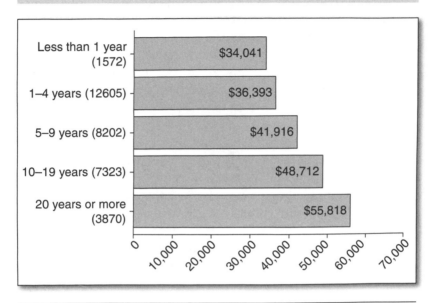

Source: Payscale (2009).

Note: Currency: U.S. dollars; Updated: May 5, 2009; Individuals reporting: 33,572.

increases in health-care premiums and nominal salary increases in contract negotiations. Often these struggles are public, with the school boards led through the lengthy process by a lawyer and teams of teachers representing themselves after teaching all day (sometimes with union support, and sometimes without). The lawyers and school board teams work together to develop the best strategy for having to pay less, to give less in terms of benefits, but the teachers are too busy teaching their children to do the same.

Glenn Sacks (2001), a former teacher and a current education and parenting columnist and radio host, noticed this pay discrepancy:

I'm not a teacher anymore because it didn't make sense to work 65 hours a week for $28,000 a year when I saw friends with the same amount of education working less hours for two or three times as much money; because rushing to before-school yard duty, lunch duty, teaching five classes, and then attending a faculty or department meeting made me feel as if I worked in a white collar sweatshop; because I spent so much time doing paperwork, yard duty, and other things that were unrelated to teaching; because I never had a moment of free time between September and June and never had a dollar in my pocket in July and August; because I spent years and thousands of dollars going to state-required, nighttime teacher-education classes that usually taught little but consumed valuable time. (para. 5)

Pay was one of the main reasons that Claire quit teaching. She says, "I couldn't support myself as a teacher. For all that low pay, there's a lot of responsibility and hours. People don't think about how long it takes to plan, prep, and grade students. I don't want to think about how many hours I work in a week." According to *Why We Teach* by Sonia Nieto (2005), teachers work an average of 50 hours a week on teaching duties, not counting any extra meetings, conferences, special events, or field trips (p. 4).

A constant theme in the interviews I conducted was the extra hours that teachers worked to be good at their jobs. They work before school, after school, and at home. Many of them take second and third jobs to support their teaching careers. As Mike said on the blog, "Pay does matter!"

Teachers do not enter the profession because of pay; however, PAY is associated with respect. If teachers made $130,000 a year, it would help greatly in people respecting them because we live in a capitalistic society. If teachers did not have to worry about surviving, they could put more energy into their jobs instead of a demeaning second job as a pizza driver. That time could be used on teaching or getting involved in the community.

It comes down to this, according to the National Education Association article "Why They Leave":

The bottom line for many educators, especially new ones, is that their income doesn't pay the rent and bills. "Teachers have to be able to afford to teach," says Johnson [a researcher with the Harvard Graduate School of Education], "Even for the most committed, the pay has to be sufficient to live a reasonable, middle class life." (Kopkowski, 2008, para. 28)

And clearly, for many educators, this simply isn't happening.

PAYING FOR SCHOOL SUPPLIES

Teachers have to get every purchase preapproved, often with a process of paperwork that can take a week or more. Educators know that the often immediate need for materials doesn't allow for teachers to use this process—not if they want to do a lab with their science class, use food in a recipe, play a review game with small rewards, or buy materials for a creative class project. Many times, the timing and process of education doesn't allow for weeks of advance time to see what materials are needed. So caring and committed teachers everywhere are dipping into their own wallets to buy what their students need. At times, it can even seem like the system is set up to support this.

In many schools, there are only a few approved vendors with accounts with the school. That means teachers have to go to specific stores, and if the supply isn't there, they have to file paperwork with administrators to see if it can be approved. In the meantime, the item is already needed. Educators often have innovative ideas about reaching their students just days before they teach a particular subject or topic. In tough economic times such as these, more and more teachers are simply not going to have the funds to buy what they need to develop innovative, creative lessons.

Cindy, from an urban middle school, said this about her hours and the costs to teachers:

Salary: You have to love this job to be in this. My day is from 7:45 to 4:00 (sometimes 5:30 p.m.). Weeknights: paperwork. Weekends: paperwork. Holidays: paperwork. Summertime: classes and workshops. I teach a subject that requires you to spend money on consumables—gloves, sugar, salt, ziptop bags, etc.—regularly. What about supplying us with $500 gift cards per year? I know some teachers spend more but it could be a start.

According to a survey in 2003 by the NEA, teachers spend an average of $433 of their own money each year (Kopkowski, 2008). While there is a tax deduction of $250 for teachers who itemize their deductions on their tax return, many educators do not know about this, or it doesn't come close to the amount they spend out of pocket each year. Edutopia staff surveyed readers about how much they reach into their own pocketbooks for supplies. Several teachers commented about this to explain their spending:[1]

Last year I bought my own Smart Board [an interactive white-board used with a computer and projector]. [I was] tired of waiting after keeping my requests to bare minimum from school and just asking for a SB for 3 years. Then our school gets a grant for SB and other materials but the grant is only for math and science classrooms. Imagine my frustration. I am 59 and use more technology in my English classroom than most other younger teachers. Teaching in a small, poor, rural school means that if I want it I have to buy it. [I] spent over $8,000 last year, but won't do that again. It's almost as if the altruistic natures of teachers and our desire to give the best to our kids enable the districts to shirk their duty. (Rho, 2008)

This shocking amount of personal spending on classroom supplies was echoed by another teacher on the blog:

I have only taught for 4 years in a Kentucky school. The districts are funded unequally, so our district gets less money and poor districts get more. In the past 4 years I have bought and paid for out of my own money: a projector, a digital camera, a document camera, and a flip video camera. I do after school tutoring, and do any professional development that pays me a stipend. I take this extra money (and more) to buy things for my classroom. If I want it, I have to buy it. My department head has taught for over 25 years and does not use technology. Therefore, she will not spend any department money on it. I buy used books from library book sales, yard sales, I volunteer at an organization that will let me then "shop" for free

---

[1] Blog quotes by Rho and Anonymous © 2008 The George Lucas Educational Foundation, www.edutopia.org. All rights reserved.

donated items. The clerks at Staples know me by sight. I go in there every time they have something free with rebate. I had to beg my department head to spend $300 a year to buy new science magazines for the kids to read. The old magazines were 10 years old. The $250 tax write-off is a joke. They should make it $1,000 a year for teachers. That MIGHT begin to cover what I spend. If I feel like I need something to do a better job of teaching I CANNOT rely on my school to purchase it for me. Sad, but true. (Anonymous, 2008)

For teachers eager to use current technology, literature, and resources to enliven and enrich their teaching, the system is broken. Many teachers want to use current technology but don't have the financial resources to make these purchases out of pocket.

A CULTURE OF DISRESPECT

Kelly stares at the paper in disbelief. On it, clearly written, and then erased, are the words, "Stupid! This is wrong! Learn how to teach!" The comment is written on a spelling assignment, where a common spelling rule is written in shorthand for the students, with a more detailed description on the back of the page. It is clear that the parent didn't even bother to read the back, or they would have understood the generalization and the assignment.

Now, Kelly has a choice. She could call this parent during her only 30-minute prep time of the day, while she should be grading or preparing for her next class, or she could simply ignore it. Kelly tries to grade a paper or two, but she can't. The comment and its disrespect deeply bother her. She reaches for the phone, leaves a message, and moves on with her day.

Later, she notices her voice-mail light is blinking. A call must have come in while she was teaching or during recess duty. The gruff voice on the phone tells her that the note shouldn't have been erased (by his son, who was probably embarrassed), that he meant for it to be read by Kelly, and he has concerns he wants to discuss with her and the principal. His tone is threatening, mocking, and disrespectful.

(Continued)

(Continued)

Kelly sighs and knows she now has to call him back, be professional and courteous even though he most certainly was not, and schedule a meeting with him and her principal during her limited personal time.

She wonders, "When did it become okay to call teachers names and threaten them? It wasn't like this when I was growing up, and that wasn't too long ago." Kelly takes a deep breath, and counts to 10 before she calls him back.

The disrespect shown to teachers in our country deeply bothers the educators I interviewed, especially those who quit. And it doesn't come only from parents but also, at times, from administrators, the general public, and the media.

Many people think that because they went to school, they are experts on education and could be great teachers. One of the reasons Melissa (a sixth-grade suburban teacher) is thinking about quitting teaching is the lack of respect she feels from her family and society. She said, "Most people think I have this cake job. My brother-in-law tells me how great he thinks I have it. He has no idea what I do, or what I deal with."

In the comments I received, teachers entwined the concept of a general lack of respect with their thoughts about pay, parents, and administrators. It surfaces throughout the chapters in this book.

Every March, in states where they vote on the school budgets (not all states do this), a very public throttling of teachers takes place. During that month, it is hard for teachers to even open up the editorial section of their local papers. Negative letters, written by local taxpayers, target teachers; the letters include misinformation (and personal insults), demonstrating a lack of understanding about teaching or how schools work. In our current economy, it is bound to get worse. People are understandably frustrated with increasing taxes, since they often have no income to spare. So who becomes the target: taxpayer-funded employees—and in March, teachers are the ones under public scrutiny. They are battling just to hold on to their benefits or to receive even a small pay increase.

It is emotionally exhausting to have your profession so publicly dragged through the mud every year. Our taxation system sets up a contentious relationship between parents, community members, and teachers; and it creates a culture of disrespect.

In an article for the *Oregonian* called "What Tired Oregon Teachers Say (When Parents Aren't Listening)," Susan Nielsen (2009) chronicles what all teachers need more of: respect, engagement, and involvement from parents. While the article brought up familiar themes—overworked parents, higher unemployment rates, and increasing rates of adversarial parent-teacher relationships—the comments posted online after the article's publication highlighted the disrespect teachers face.

The respondents berated teachers for complaining about their "cushy" jobs, stating as fact some of the myths that persist about teaching, such as teachers only work eight months a year, six hours a day, with full pensions and a guaranteed 5 percent raise each year. The negative tone, verging on disdain, in many of the over 250 responses was striking. The article wasn't even about teacher benefits or pay, but that's what the online forum turned into. Here is one individual noticing the very same thing:

> When did this article become focused on teacher pay and/or benefits? EVERY time there is an article about teaching, the topic is always turned inside out and upside down so the focus shifts to compensation and the "greedy" teachers and their evil union. THAT is the problem here. (Orteacher, 2009)

On websites and blogs, in editorial pages and in the hallways, teachers are noticing an increase in the lack of respect for teachers.

Mike sums up why he quit teaching:

> In conclusion I left because of a lack of respect for the profession. People say they respect it. They need to put their money where their mouth is. Now I work half as hard, get twice the pay, more respect, and I can feel safe at work.

THE MARTYR SYSTEM: DO MORE FOR FREE

Teachers are asked to give more and more of their personal time, without compensation. They are asked to participate in committees that meet outside of schooltime; to take classes over the summer, at night, and on weekends (their unpaid time); and to host multiple parent nights, overnight field trips, and other activities that are not compensated. Most teachers want to meet with parents, go on exciting field trips with their students, and take professional development courses to improve and enrich their teaching. To ask educators to do these things continually without compensation is disrespectful and actually stifles teacher creativity and innovation. Teachers are dedicated to the lives of all children, including their own. These constant demands take away from their own families as well.

Principals and administrators pass along course posting after course posting, some giving verbal and written pressure (or directives) for teachers to take these classes or attend conferences. Yes, teachers are lifelong learners, and of course they want to grow and learn from current research. But in what other field are you expected to donate your unpaid vacation time to take classes and, in many cases, pay for your own textbooks? Some salaried positions come with expected overtime without pay, but what is unique to teaching is that the pay rate is so low to begin with. Nurses, police officers, and state workers are only a few examples of workers who are paid overtime for their work beyond eight hours a day.

The culture of asking for more, which I call the martyr system, begins early. As a new teacher in a district, it is common for principals to tell the teacher they need this sort of training and that, and the new teacher is expected to complete the coursework, or get off on the wrong foot in their school. So right away, new teachers spend their summers taking courses to prepare for the school year, before they are even on the payroll. New teachers learn quickly that if they want to be successful, they have to volunteer their personal time before even setting foot in the school as a teacher.

Here is an example of the martyr system at work. A teacher was required to go to the new-employee orientation even though he had been a teacher in that same school the year before (he was working under a different contract during a teacher exchange). He knew the staff, the schedule, and the students. He had ample experience as a teacher. He knew that this wasn't in the contract, and they weren't going to pay him to go. This teacher had to plan for child care for his two young children. When he asked the coordinator of the program if it was a contractual paid day, she said that no one else had ever asked her that. Now, would a brand-new teacher or employee want to make waves and bring up this unpaid training day? No, because they are just starting out and are overwhelmed to begin with. For years, new teachers had completed this volunteer day to begin their teaching careers. But this teacher saw this as a lack of respect, and he filed a grievance. As a result, the policy was changed because it wasn't allowed in the contract.

Abby, who quit teaching elementary school music in 2005, shared a telling comparison in our interview about her new job with the state:

> While teaching, I was very sad and resentful that I gave so much from 8 to 5 that I was physically and emotionally exhausted when I got home. Since resigning from teaching, I have learned that the rest of the work world is accepting of "personal time," does not expect you to take phone calls at any hour of the day or night at home, lets you use the bathroom at your leisure, and realizes that if you do not finish your work during the 8-hour workday, you simply had too much work or should be paid overtime to finish it.

These issues may seem trivial to an outsider looking in on the world of education, but they are not. The cumulative effect of low salaries, the constant pressure to give more, and personal spending on classroom supplies combine to make teachers feel unvalued and disrespected. Is this how we want to treat the dedicated individuals who spend their days with our children and impart the skills they need to navigate the world? We all need to analyze our educational communities through the lens of this martyr syndrome and lack of professional compensation—school by school, person by person—and realize, we must all work together to create the most healthful, positive, and engaging environment possible for the teachers as well as students in America's schools.

you can... DO IT! RECOMMENDATIONS FOR ADMINISTRATORS AND TEACHER LEADERS

• Support teachers as they work for professional pay. In conversations with community and school board members, explain how more pay shows teachers more respect and value and can increase teacher retention.

• Establish a principal's discretionary fund that has roughly $500 in it per class. This could be used on an as-needed basis without an extensive approval process for classroom materials.

• Team with the administrative and district staff to streamline the purchase-order approval process and work to make purchasing current technology, literature, and resources easier and more available for teachers.

• Value teachers' time and personal life. Schedule meetings during the school workday and hold as few staff meetings as possible while retaining good communication. Offer to compensate teachers (on a per diem basis), or give them release time for extra work outside of school on special projects and for time spent in courses or workshops.

• At the beginning of the year, as a staff, create a grid of the committee responsibilities for the school. Eliminate any that aren't essential to the functioning of the school, and consolidate any committees that have similar goals. Then, work together to assign duties as equally as possible and to schedule committee meetings during inservice times to lessen the impact on students and on teachers' personal time.

• Try to make sure that no personal bias or philosophy is getting in the way of purchase approvals.

• Consider the impacts of ideas and requests, and think creatively. A math night sounds wonderful for students and parents. Maybe an early release day for students or no staff meeting one morning would work as a respectful way to compensate for that time.

 ## WORDS OF WISDOM FROM VETERAN TEACHERS

One recurring idea that many veteran teachers shared was for all teachers to learn to be very selective about when they say yes. Without being negative, these teachers are simply saying no to more work without compensation and selecting only what is most meaningful to their teaching. They advocate for meetings to be completed during school hours, if possible, and for the staff to free each other up as necessary to attend them. As team players and direct communicators, veteran teachers try not to let the pressure get to them personally and handle each situation directly without being defensive.

Many veteran teachers are members of the teachers' union and volunteer countless hours to negotiate new contracts in their districts. This is not an easy process, involving late-night meetings, savvy lawyers working for the school boards, and sometimes demeaning commentary. But they keep at it, working for more professional salaries and better working conditions. Knowing they are forwarding the goals of the profession is worthy and helps them feel valuable.

Other teachers are working hard to elect public officials who value education. One special educator voiced the following opinion:

To attract greater numbers of quality people and keep quality professionals, we need to *pay* quality people to join and stay in this profession. Life is about choices. Our government and communities have made the choice to chronically underfund public education. We pour money into national security, tax cuts for the wealthy, and any number of other pet projects. It is simply not true that we cannot afford to put more money into education. We have chosen for years to underfund public education (including special education, which has never come close to being funded as it was intended by law). The United States has the money; it is a matter of how we choose to spend it.

This teacher shared (as did many others) that he is politically active and committed to voting for school board members, and local and national officials, who will value and fund public education, and they encourage others to do the same.

SUCCESS STORIES: A DECENT WORKING WAGE

Veteran teacher Melanie feels lucky. In her college town, people in the corporate world are losing their jobs. Even though she's been behind them in salary for years, Melanie is finally catching up. After teaching for 20 years, she makes almost $100,000. From her humble beginnings as a first-year teacher making $10,000 a year, she is proud that her school community decided teachers should be as respected and well compensated as many other working professionals, and though it was not an easy journey, they arrived at this point nonetheless.

Melanie knows that she works at least a full-time equivalent just like any working professional, but her schedule is spread out differently through the year (NEA, 2009a). She works overtime in September and October getting her classroom going; during report-card, progress-report, and parent-conference times; and during special events spread throughout the school year.

Melanie knows when she retires, she will be just fine. Not rich, by any stretch of the imagination, but livable, manageable, and able to do some things she has always wanted to. And for this, at this point in our nation's history, she feels lucky.

HOPE ON THE HORIZON: TEACHER PAY AND RESPECT IN NEW YORK AND OTHER STATES

Teacher salaries vary widely across the United States (see Table 5.1 on page 92). Recently, a story ran in the *New York Times* (Winerip, 2009) about the exceptional teachers' salaries in some New York areas and how this is increasing respect and interest in teaching. One veteran teacher in an urban school was described as making over $100,000, and she has job security, health care, and retirement benefits—none of which are a given in our current economy. Another teacher, in the same school, making over $100,000 shared how people viewed her differently than they had before:

> Marie Costanza, 53, another 100K teacher here, said people are suddenly looking at her and her teacher-husband differently. "Friends in the corporate world who used to belittle teaching—they're panicky, they don't know what to do," said Ms. Costanza, who made $6,850 starting out in 1977. "My husband and I have had private conversations about how nice it is knowing that we have our security." (para. 8)

The change in attitude toward teaching as a profession, because of the increase in salary, is clear to this veteran teacher:

> Before this recession hit, said Gaya Shakes, 56, 101K, "people would be like, 'Oh you're just a teacher.' Now you hear, 'How do I get on the substitute's list?'" (Winerip, 2009, para. 9)

The issues of respect and compensation go hand in hand. According to the *New York Times* article, schools in New Jersey and Connecticut have similar pay scales.

The Economic Policy Institute addresses the connection between compensation, teacher recruitment, and teacher retention (Allegretto, Corcoran, & Mishel, 2008):

> Raising teacher compensation is a critical component in any strategy to recruit and retain a higher quality teacher workforce if the goal is to affect the broad array of teachers—that is, move the quality of the median teacher. Policies that solely focus on changing the composition of the current compensation levels, such as merit or pay-for-performance schemes, are unlikely to be effective unless they also correct the teacher compensation disadvantage in the labor market. (p. 2)

States such as California, New York, Connecticut, and New Jersey demonstrate their high commitment to paying their teachers as professionals. In doing so, they increase respect for

Table 5.1   Average salaries ($) of public school teachers, 2007–2008

Rank	State	2007–2008
1	California	64,424
2	New York	62,332
3	Connecticut	61,976
4	New Jersey	61,277
5	District Of Columbia	60,628
6	Illinois	60,474
7	Massachusetts	60,471
8	Maryland	60,069
9	Rhode Island	57,168
10	Alaska	56,758
11	Michigan	56,096
12	Delaware	55,994
13	Pennsylvania	55,833
14	Ohio	53,410
15	Hawaii	53,400
16	Wyoming	53,074
	United States	52,308
17	Oregon	51,811
18	Georgia	51,560
19	Minnesota	50,582
20	Washington	49,884
21	Wisconsin	49,051
22	Indiana	48,508
23	Nevada	47,710
24	New Hampshire	47,609

Rank	State	2007–2008
25	North Carolina	47,354
26	Colorado	47,248
27	Kentucky	47,207
28	Louisiana	46,964
29	Florida	46,930
30	Virginia	46,796
31	Iowa	46,664
32	Alabama	46,604
33	Vermont	46,593
34	Texas	46,179
35	Arkansas	45,773
36	Arizona	45,772
37	South Carolina	45,758
38	Kansas	45,136
39	New Mexico	45,112
40	Tennessee	45,030
41	Idaho	44,099
42	Oklahoma	43,551
43	Maine	43,397
44	Missouri	43,206
45	Nebraska	42,885
46	Montana	42,874
47	West Virginia	42,529
48	Mississippi	42,403
49	Utah	41,615
50	North Dakota	40,279
51	South Dakota	36,674

Source: NEA (2008).

teachers and move teaching toward other professional occupations in salary. Two teachers from New York shared that their higher salaries result in increased productivity and positive feelings about their communities and profession:

> When you feel appreciated and respected by the community, you want to do a great job and everyone benefits (teachers, students, and parents). The bottom line is, when you feel valued you want to go above and beyond the call of duty. In addition, making a good salary enables a teacher to live in the community where he/she teaches. This provides a sense of community for all. When teachers feel connected to the community, they take pride in their work. They want their neighborhood schools to be successful.

Another New York educator shared the positive effect that professional pay for educators has:

> The true reward from teaching comes from the students. However, if we were not paid reasonably well, we would get the feeling that the community does not value our efforts as well as understand the difficulty and importance of what we do as teachers every day. When you feel appreciated, it affects your whole demeanor in a positive way that is noticed by your students as well as your colleges.

This is powerful. These educators noticed the significant impact their compensation has on their motivation, positive feelings about school, and their interactions with students.

THE SILVER LINING: HELPING CHILDREN LEARN AND GROW

Teachers find the intrinsic rewards of teaching to be worth much more than money. There is nothing more rewarding for teachers than to see the face of a student light up when they finally understand something. It may be a physics problem, the addition of two-digit numbers, or reading a word. That utter joy and delight in sharing, "I did it!" with the person you helped is absolutely a sustaining factor in teaching. We crave it, late into the night, early in the morning, and in between, pondering how we can help little Joey understand new material.

Julia knows this. She teaches in a rural, poverty-ridden school. "Since I work with mainly at-risk and remedial students," she said, "I've gotten to see some kids really make gains that made me feel like what I was doing was worth getting up in the morning for." This is why many teachers still teach. There is simply more work to be done, more kids to help, more learning to make happen.

Amy is a teacher we can't afford to lose. She teaches in the inner city, with students who desperately need her guidance:

> I continue to teach because I love working with the students and when I see that student succeed or that I somehow made a difference, I say to myself, "This is why I love my job." I have only been teaching for about 4 years and the only thing that has changed is that I am starting to feel the burnout (long hours and stress).

Amy wants to continue making a difference in these kids' lives, where they have challenges many of us can't even begin to understand. She needs the support of her school and community, so she can sustain a career in education.

An elementary special educator with nine years experience put it succinctly:

> I teach because I love to work with kids. I love to see the progress they make and that gleam in their eye when they learn something new. I love to see my student who fliply tells me, "I don't think I'll come to school Monday. My dad says I can stay home and play video games." And, yes, his dad really does let him. I tell him that he is important to me and that I'll be looking for him. I love to see his grin on Monday when he's standing in his classroom, wondering if I'll really notice that he's there. I notice. Making a difference; not making a bottom line. That's why I'm there.

Teachers want better pay, but they also know that isn't what life is all about. They want to make a difference in their students' lives, both personally and academically. This teacher noticing that student may have changed the course of his life. She might never know, but she has to believe in her heart that by noticing, caring, and teaching him every day, she's made a difference. And that is worth more than any CEO makes.

ADDITIONAL RESOURCES

Print Resources

Crosby, B. (2003). *$100,000 teacher: A solution to America's declining public school system.* Sterling, VA: Capital Books.

Little, C., Gareis, C., & Stronge, J. (2006). *Teacher pay and teacher quality: Attracting, developing, and retaining the best teachers.* Thousand Oaks, CA: Corwin.

Odden, A., & Kelley, C. (2001). *Paying teachers for what they know and do.* Thousand Oaks, CA: Corwin.

Internet Resources

National Educational Association, Professional Pay Resources

National Educational Association. (n.d.). *Professional pay.* Available from www.nea.org/home/ProfessionalPay.html

Myths and Facts About Educator Pay

National Educational Association. (2009). *Myths and facts about educator pay.* Available from www.nea.org/home/12661.htm

Professional Compensation for Educators

American Federation of Teachers. (2002). *Professional compensation for teachers.* Available from http://archive.aft.org/about/resolutions/2002/compensation.htm (an article that describes ways to implement additional pay options and other comprehensive compensation improvement ideas)

CHAPTER SIX

Parents

The mother of one of her students stands in the classroom. The morning bell has rung, and she is talking loudly about her child's boredom with school. Third- and fourth-grade students are milling about the room, getting materials, talking, laughing, and finding their seats for a class meeting. Marilyn, the teacher, is trying to set up materials for her math class and help her students get ready for the day. The parent, looking for the direct engagement of the teacher, doesn't realize how busy the morning is, or doesn't care. "She just knows most of what everyone is teaching her—and this school has done nothing about it. What do you plan on doing to engage her more?" Marilyn's eyes flicker from the woman to Connor, who is pushing Henry. She glares at them over the mom's shoulder, her pulse quickening with the stress of the situation. She needs to go give her students directions, start morning meeting, and check in with her students about their homework and other needs that pop up every day. Marilyn nods, breathes as deeply as she can before explaining herself, her program, and the school again to this particular parent, while the students continue unsupervised and in need of her leadership.

Variations of this scene play themselves out every day in our schools. A small number of challenging parents like this one can have an inordinate impact on the best teachers and on the education of other children. It doesn't have to be this way. Let's take a look at a situation where the parents and the teacher are in a positive partnership.

Across the hall from Marilyn, a parent stops by after school as third-grade teacher Lynne is busily setting up for the next day. She stops and goes to the door, without anxiety, because this parent has always treated her with respect, even when they discuss challenging and difficult issues. The parent says, "I know you are busy, but I want to touch base with you at some point about Sam's project. When would be a good time to talk?" Lynne knows she can either make time to talk with the parent now or schedule a meeting, based on what works for both of their schedules. Just this simple disarming question from the parent, which shows an understanding that Lynne has a life, a schedule, and family obligations, sets her at ease. "Come in," the teacher says, "I have a few minutes before I need to pick up my son. Tell me how Sam's project is coming along." The tone is now set for a positive, productive meeting.

Many people reading this book are probably wishing for *any* parental involvement in their schools. Especially in our nation's neediest schools, parents are often too busy working multiple jobs (just to feed their families) to be as involved as they might like in the schooling of their children. Some parents are simply unavailable due to drug and alcohol abuse, or mental illness (Gomby & Hsieh, n.d.). This is a huge problem that has been widely acknowledged. Research tells us that the more involved and invested a parent is in the child's education, the more successful the child will be (Jeynes, 2005)—and all educators want that (see Figure 6.1). Nonetheless, a problem that consistently came up in my interviews with disenchanted teachers was the serious challenge of interacting with disrespectful parents.

Figure 6.1   Processes of family involvement and elementary school
children's outcomes

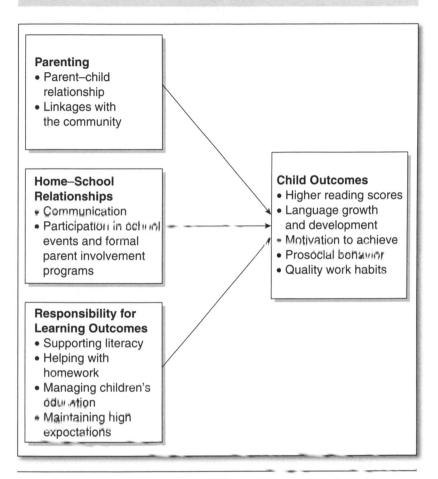

Source: From "Family Involvement in Elementary School Children's Education," by M. Caspe, M. E. Lopez, and C. Wolos, Winter 2006/2007, *Family Involvement Makes a Difference,* 2, p. 2. Reprinted with permission from Harvard Family Research Project.

UNREALISTIC DEMANDS AND NO LIMITS

It's his last parent conference for the night, and it is scheduled to last 20 minutes. It's now 8 p.m., and he's been at school since 7 a.m. Chris, a sixth-grade teacher, is thorough, efficient, and ready to share his

(Continued)

(Continued)

notes about a student in this next parent conference. An hour later, he hasn't eaten dinner or seen his newborn baby, and he's being asked what psychologists he studied in college and to defend the problems of public education. Chris has shared detailed information about this child's progress, despite his fatigue; but to her parents, he is simply the face of all that is wrong with public education. It is understandable that Chris feels as though his professionalism is being attacked.

It seems that, in every community, there is a small group of parents who know no limits when dealing with teachers. They will come into a classroom at any time—during tests or prep periods or in the middle of a lesson—and demand one-on-one attention. This usually happens when they are upset about something and want to address it immediately. Some parents jump over the teacher and talk to the principal about classroom issues that are better handled by the parent and the teacher together. If a teacher has several challenging parents like this in one class, the cumulative effects can be serious. The stress of difficult conversations can take an emotional, as well as a physical, toll.

The problem of overly demanding and aggressive parents surfaced in many of my interviews. Karen, a special educator, describes her struggles with parent-teacher communications:

There is a distinct feeling of mistrust among some parents, where they always believe what their child says over their teacher. They assume that teaching is not that hard and that they could do it better. Be my guest. These same parents want to have hour-long conversations on the phone and send you daily e-mails micromanaging their child and his or her education. One parent regularly sent me daily e-mails, often with long articles and attachments to read. I remember the day she sent me several e-mails with attachments totaling over 300 pages specifically related to her son's needs. Can you say "over the top"?

Communicating with parents regularly is part of a teacher's job, of course, and is crucial in developing a working relationship to support the child. Good teachers regularly e-mail, call, post Internet pages, and send newsletters or notes to communicate issues pertaining to school. But a new crop of parents is demanding personal e-mails, calls, or meetings on a weekly, and sometimes on a daily, basis. If teachers were working with three children, perhaps this would be possible. In a class of 25 or more students, this is unrealistic. And often, a parent demanding this kind of attention will get it, taking away from the educational time for the other 24 students in the class.

One elementary teacher described a student who lost a jacket at school, and the mother called her and yelled into her voice mail that she would have to pay for the jacket if it was not found. The teacher described how this happened with various clothing items over the year:

> While I can sympathize with her about her son's disorganization, and the finances of dressing children, where is the accountability for the child? The items were found every time, usually by the child, and there was never a word from the parent, or an apology. I just don't know how teachers came to be responsible for not only the education of their students, but also the management of all their students' stuff.

Teachers are working to build organizational and social skills that foster independence and responsible decision making. What kind of message are we sending our kids in these situations about personal responsibility?

MY CHILD IS ALWAYS RIGHT

Colby is a smart cookie. She has *almost* been caught by numerous teachers for bullying another student. In notes, whispered comments, on the basketball court, and in the classroom, Colby is clever about how and when to make other girls feel small. Throughout the year, the teacher and the guidance counselor have spent many hours proactively working with Colby to develop better social and coping skills. The teacher has worked hard to connect personally with her and build a strong relationship. Colby is slippery—hard to catch, but after several months, finally, several other students and teachers speak up about what they have seen and heard. The principal and guidance counselor have taken copious notes and cross-checked their information with other students, to make sure that it is accurate. Nonetheless, when the mom is called in to talk about the situation, she is defensive, irate, and convinced, even after all the evidence presented, that the school is singling out her child for punishment for no real reason.

Parents want to protect their children and to believe in them at all times. But some parents seem to confuse constantly defending their child's behavior with loving their child. Even if it is obvious that their child has done something wrong, some parents will defend them no matter what. As I interviewed teachers, this frustrating problem came up again and again. Many of us grew up in a time when teachers were given the benefit of the doubt and were accorded some reasonable respect for their judgment. Of course it is important for parents to listen to their child's perspective and experiences at school. What seems to be lacking, however, is an understanding of children's development and the importance of role models. When children learn that parents will take their side on any issue, they can learn to manipulate situations to their advantage. After all, most kids have a primary objective of not getting in trouble. Some children learn how to take a situation at school and explain it in a way that will upset the parent, so that action is taken. This parent will then call the teacher, irate; and the child might feel satisfied and smug at the retribution. What kind of modeling is this for behavior? The lesson the child learns is to manipulate, to gain revenge and push the blame and accountability onto others. This can quickly turn children into adults who make poor health, relationship, and life choices. It is absolutely crucial to model and maintain positive and productive partnerships between parents and teachers in schools. Parents and teachers are all there to help children learn and grow into responsible adults who can work with others in challenging situations.

Laura's main reason for quitting teaching is clear:

I quit due to lack of parental support and parental harassment. It is hard enough to do your job and be the best teacher without "Joe's" parents constantly questioning why their child is getting negative comments about behavior and/or that child is failing because they fail to be involved in class and/or do assignments. They feel that I must be wrong, because their spoiled, violent, and incredibly rude child is an ANGEL and there is no way on Earth they could possibly behave the way I describe. Even when the parent sees it themselves, they ignore it and then wonder why their child is in jail, is pregnant, and/or is on drugs, or the like by the time they are 14. If the parent shows no respect for the teacher, why should their child?

While frank and harshly expressed, this troubling comment shines a light on a significant, recurring difficulty (and source of frustration) for teachers.

HELICOPTER PARENTS: MICROMANAGING THE CLASSROOM

It's Diana's first year of teaching. She works at least 50 hours a week, learning the ropes from a veteran teacher; learning about her students, the community, the curriculum; and creating meaningful learning activities for her students. On this particular day as she faces her fifth graders and gets organized to begin math class, one student hands her a note from his dad.

Diana opens it as her class is finding their seats. It is a graded assignment that she handed back yesterday. The paper is filled with red writing. Notes are all over the paper where Diana wrote comments about the child's work: angry words questioning her judgment, grade, criteria, and teaching. Her face grows prickly and hot. She is rattled. No one has ever written anything like this to her before, and she wonders if the parent is right, if she is cut out for teaching after all. Diana sets the letter on her desk, and as she turns back to the class to begin teaching, she notices her hand shaking. The grade on the student's assignment? An A minus.

Diana spends hours after school writing this parent a point-by-point letter defending her grade, her teaching, and her assignment.

Every teacher has experienced a moment like this. The incidence of micromanaging students' grades, the assignments, and the teachers in general is a growing problem. The *New York Times'* Well blog (Pope, 2008) cited a study published in the journal *Anxiety, Stress, & Coping,* which followed the stress level of 20-year veteran teachers in Germany. The study found that the greatest pressure that led to teacher burnout came from parents. Many of the comments on the post were from former teachers who suffered intense pressure and even bullying behaviors from parents. One high school teacher described problems after reorganizing the English literature course offerings:

> About fifteen parents demanded that I call them every day and report back their students' performance for the day. Other parents were overly aggressive, demanding that I meet with them in a conference before school at least once a week. In these conferences, I would be subjected to their angry diatribe; they felt that their child's poor performance was my fault—they didn't want him placed in "standard" and had demanded he be put in the "honors" track. While I believe every student should have the opportunity to challenge themselves in their coursework that does not give them or their parents the right to blame others if they do not experience the success they wish. One particularly memorable line, when I requested we meet after school one week as opposed to 6:30 a.m., was that "We are professionals, and we cannot meet with you then." I wondered to myself, "And what am I?" (Catherine, 2008, para. 3)

Teachers fear they might be sued or fired if they do not conform to a parent's request, even when the teacher's actions are educationally sound, reasonable, and responsible. Another teacher who commented on the *New York Times'* Well blog left teaching because of this pressure:

> I spent only one and a half years teaching high school. The students were never the problem. The parents and a nonsupportive school administration drove me out. . . . When a student did not achieve an acceptable grade, it was always the teacher's fault. Parents could and do bully administrators to have the grade changed for them to an acceptable level. Here in our district that has happened with somewhat dire consequences to the teacher.

I'm much more content teaching college levels. Students are at a level where they have to accept responsibility for their own actions. Parents have less influence. My job is not in jeopardy because of what the student earns as a grade. (Barrientos, 2008, para. 1)

Good teachers know they need to inform parents and students about the grading process. Current professional development and teacher literature tells teachers to explain how assignments will be graded, explicitly communicating rubric goals or other grading methods to students. Many teachers send information home about grading practices and policies, as well. But teachers are driven out of teaching because of relentless and public questioning of assigned grades:

I taught for almost ten years but left the classroom for the very reason stated above—parents. I loved the students I taught, I loved my subject I taught, but I hated the constant questions from parents about why a child got a B or C, how can they fail even though they never did any work, and why didn't the test come home the next day. Every now and then I wanted a night off from grading, but with the e-mails, and phone calls to not only me but the principal, I just could not do it any more. I loved the parents who were reasonable, who looked at the assignments and made their children do them. I never minded answering how I arrived at a grade, but those parents who believed Cs were failing and As were the only acceptable grade drove me from a career I loved. (Andrea, 2008, para. 1)

In smaller schools, this type of parenting, often referred to as helicopter parenting, can affect the very configuration of classrooms, assignments, and curriculum. In one small suburban school where I interviewed teachers, a group of parents believed their children were gifted. Many of the students were indeed high-level learners in the school but hadn't been identified as gifted, which usually only refers to 3 to 5 percent of the school population (Florida State University, 2009). The students' learning needs were met through differentiated instruction within the classroom, a model that had been successful for high-level learners for years. But this group of parents repeatedly met with the principal and the teachers, demanding ability-level groups. One teacher explained how this played out:

> After a whole school year of phone calls, e-mails, classroom interruptions, being cornered at school events, and pressure from my administrator, I wore down. We changed the whole structure of our classrooms based on the persistent pressure from a small group of parents. Was it better for all of our students? Probably not.

10 Things Schools/Teachers Wish Parents Would Do

1. Establish a daily family routine, including healthy eating and sleeping habits.

2. Build their child's self-esteem by expressing interest in the child's schoolwork and affirming the child's worth through positive messages.

3. Communicate openly with the school and contact the school when they are aware of issues concerning their child's school success.

4. Set high and realistic standards for their child.

5. Check on homework regularly and ask questions about their child's work.

6. Read or talk with their child. Connect everyday experiences to what is being learned in school.

7. Express high but realistic expectations for their child.

8. Use community learning opportunities. Expose their child to the library, museums, the theater, concerts, etc. Encourage their child to join clubs, scouts, afterschool sports or fine arts, and other community programs.

9. Monitor out-of-school activities and set expectations for appropriate behavior.

10. Model learning at home by playing games, reading newspapers or magazines, and discussing current events.

Parents and teachers have the unique and powerful opportunity to develop a strong, supportive relationship that can motivate and inspire children to do great things. We owe it to them and to ourselves to find ways to build positive partnerships and a respectful climate. By doing so, we not only can give our children the best education possible, but we also increase the likelihood that teachers will stay in the field doing what they do best.

you can... DO IT! RECOMMENDATIONS FOR ADMINISTRATORS AND TEACHER LEADERS

- Commit to establishing a climate that fosters clear communication and avenues for dialogue between parents and teachers (between students and teachers, and between educators). How do you do this?

- Establish a schoolwide approach to communication. Educate staff, students, and parents on the standards used to communicate, for example, "We will treat each other with respect." In all communications, staff needs to speak up and support team members by calling out behavior that is not respectful.

In one school I researched, they developed school norms. (See Example of School Norms.) Norms can be developed by staff or by teams consisting of parents and staff, where members of the team agree to the norms. Norms are reviewed at the beginning of each meeting (including parent-teacher meetings, Educational Support Team, and Individualized Education Plan meetings, as well as most staff meetings).

Example of School Norms

1. We will create a safe place for people to speak honestly, respectfully, and constructively.

2. We will treat each other with respect.

3. We believe that parents are active and informed partners in their child's education.

(Continued)

(Continued)

4. We will acknowledge and appreciate the hard work and achievements of our students.

5. We will try to follow best meeting practices:

   ➢ Provide essential data or report
   ➢ Arrive on time
   ➢ Utilize a timekeeper
   ➢ Follow an agenda
   ➢ Follow through on action steps
   ➢ End on time

   As members of the school community and role models for our students, we will demonstrate cooperation, responsibility, respect, encouragement, and accountability.

   Source: Rumney Memorial School (2008b).

- At the beginning of the year, establish school protocols and policies for communicating. Setting up clear expectations for parents is a critical first step for administrators and teachers. In school and classroom communications, it needs to be clear to parents, as well as students and teachers, what their responsibilities are. Institute steps for communicating: Clarify times and outline the avenues for parent-teacher contact, for example, open house, parent-teacher conferences, and additional times by appointment. Following are some suggested guidelines:

1. Please feel free to contact the teacher via e-mail or phone message to set up a meeting about any behavioral, social, or academic concerns.

2. Be aware that a teacher has few opportunities to correspond during a school day and may have family responsibilities that limit communication from home. Please allow a few days for a response.

3. Meetings about a student are best set up in advance. Teachers are busy planning, preparing, and delivering

quality education for all students and need to focus on that task during the day. They would be glad to set up a meeting with a parent at a convenient time for both parties.

4. If a parent has a problem or concern, please communicate first directly with the teacher. This helps parents and teachers develop a positive relationship to support the student.

5. If at any time a parent is upset about a situation at school, please remember to communicate respectfully, so all parties can work together in productive problem solving.

• Communicate policies to staff, to students, and to parents. Handbooks, newsletters, websites, information sessions, even hallways, are good places to clarify and role model good communication. Both administrators and teachers should play a part in the effort to educate.

Clarify responsibilities of all parties: At open house, teachers can share guidelines to follow for parent and school communications. By making these clear, and stating them proactively, you can head off some potential problems. Then, refer to the guidelines when working with parents. Include information about what happens when a discipline or behavioral infraction occurs—or when homework is not turned in or school days are missed—and how it is handled. This could be in the parent handbook and on the website.

• Support and enforce policies as much as possible. Principals can start this by communicating respect for educators and their time: Teachers are busy planning and teaching children, and they need the respect to do that as fully as they can. If a parent has an issue or concerns, please e-mail or call the teacher, and allow them time to respond. Most teachers can barely find time to go to the bathroom during the school day so expecting an immediate response is not realistic. And the principal can convey the benefits of reading the communications from school to stay informed.

Walk the halls, if necessary, to guide parents out of classrooms during important instruction time (unless they are volunteering), so teachers can get back to teaching. Establish a sign-in policy for all visitors (even school board members): This way, the principal will know whether a parent is volunteering, picking up their child, or possibly interrupting a class lesson. Except in certain circumstances, such as an emergency situation, parents who continually drop in unannounced can be guided to make an appointment; or teachers can be contacted by staff to verify whether a drop-in visit is convenient at this time; or a message can be conveyed by staff to the teacher or student as needed.

• Provide backup and support for teachers. During parent conferences, the principal should be onsite to assist with difficult situations that might arise. In one online forum for principals, veteran administrators shared this advice:

I usually sit with all the teachers individually before conferences and ask if there are any tricky ones or if the teachers want me to sit in on any," replied one online mentor. "What I have been doing for the past couple of years during parent-teacher conferences," replied another online correspondent, "is making myself available in a central area. . . . I have the recent assessment/testing data with me and I encourage parents to sit with me." (Curtis, 2002, para. 12)

• Mediate challenging conferences with parents. In addition to sharing information about parent responsibilities and respectful communication in newsletters, speeches, and on the website, the principal could agree to meet with parents who show a continual pattern of extreme behaviors. The principal, possibly in conjunction with the superintendent or guidance counselor, could clearly convey the school community's expectations for good communication. The list of extremely challenging parents is usually not too long, so a principal could make a real difference by targeting specific parents for this kind of work. It could simply be a meeting to review the communication guidelines, indicating that this year is a fresh start, and to set a positive tone for the year.

• Help teachers be more assertive in their dealings. Support teachers when they encourage parents to follow the policy: Teachers are busy planning and teaching children, and they need the respect to do that as fully as they can. In Marilyn's situation, she could have said, "I really can't talk right now; I need to help my students. Jot me a note or call me if you'd like to discuss this later." And she could've walked away, putting a period on the conversation. To do this in a vacuum, though, without the principal's support would put her at risk of being thought less of by a powerful, vocal parent.

Work out language for teachers to communicate when asked about a personal issue by a parent. If everyone says it, and stands by it, overreaching parents will get the message. For example, staff could decide to use language such as "I'm not comfortable discussing that, but I am happy to schedule time with you when we can discuss your child's progress."

At a staff meeting, or during an inservice, role-play parent-teacher meetings with classroom teachers, especially focusing on handling difficult issues and situations. Role playing would not only help teachers to formulate thoughts but also to practice respectful ways to voice them. A role-play partner could help decide on language to use, anticipate parent responses, and in general, prepare the teacher for the discussion. Confidence gained in a role-play situation can, perhaps, carry into the real situation. Teachers could even bring a current problem or issue they plan to share during an upcoming parent-teacher conference, making this practice immediately relevant and useful.

- Take preventative measures. Develop parenting classes or information sessions about handling a child's behavioral issues. The guidance counselor could receive a stipend (from grants, fundraising, or a community fund) to lead a series of workshops where role playing difficult conversations with children, teachers, and school officials are practiced. With some community support and planning, child care could be offered, so families could more likely attend these workshops, and they could be held at times when busy working parents could attend.

Teach the parents: Share the classroom policies and standards with parents. Educate parents on using the responsive-classroom approach (Northeast Foundation for Children, 2010), which is "an approach to elementary teaching that emphasizes social, emotional, and academic growth in a strong and safe school community." These strategies are good for all ages, and parents will learn how to support students in making good decisions.

- Troubleshoot. When a breakdown of polite communication happens, both parties need to recognize it as such, and communicate so it won't happen again. A strong school leader who is informed of a challenging parent situation should take the lead as the liaison between the teacher and the parent. The principal should reaffirm the parameters for good communication and reframe the discussion so that all parties are working for the benefit of the child.

If parents ignore their responsibilities, or expect too much, the school community needs to identify the problem and create ways to help the parent. Help the parent develop a better understanding of respectful communication protocols and practices that support education. Problems can frequently be avoided by clarifying expectations upfront. And parents who struggle with their responsibilities for legitimate reasons can be put in contact with community and school resources.

- Don't forget the students! Many older students are aware how their interactions at home with parents can inflame a situation at school. Enlist the help of a guidance counselor at the beginning of the year and lead group discussions about communicating; cover communicating issues from home to school. Lead students in role-playing, casting students as parents, teachers, and students.

Read through the parent expectations with the class and develop student expectations for communication, as well. Have a student write these expectations on poster board and display them in the classroom. Or write them together, and have the teacher and students sign them as a classroom contract.

Decide on a classroom philosophy. Many schools use the responsive-classroom approach (Northeast Foundation for Children, 2010). Designed to empower kids to value and respect their classroom and school community, the program entails specific classroom practices that encourage and support students to make good decisions based on their impact on others:

Morning Meeting—gathering as a whole class each morning to greet one another, share news, and warm up for the day ahead

Rule Creation—helping students create classroom rules to ensure an environment that allows all class members to meet their learning goals

Interactive Modeling—teaching children to notice and internalize expected behaviors through a unique modeling technique

Positive Teacher Language—using words and tone as a tool to promote children's active learning, sense of community, and self-discipline

Logical Consequences—responding to misbehavior in a way that allows children to fix and learn from their mistakes while preserving their dignity

Guided Discovery—introducing classroom materials using a format that encourages independence, creativity, and responsibility

Academic Choice—increasing student learning by allowing students teacher-structured choices in their work

Classroom Organization—setting up the physical room in ways that encourage students' independence, cooperation, and productivity

Working With Families—creating avenues for hearing parents' insights and helping them understand the school's teaching approaches

Collaborative Problem Solving—using conferencing, role playing, and other strategies to resolve problems with students (Northeast Foundation for Children, 2010, para. 5)

Most important, model good communication and stress management, with other staff, the parents, and the students, in everyday interactions.

WORDS OF WISDOM FROM VETERAN TEACHERS

The veteran teachers I spoke with had several ideas for how to work with challenging parents. Through the years, they developed a positive, direct, and concise way of communicating. They set communication parameters at the beginning of the school year and were direct and clear about the best way to reach them.

Veteran teachers who are successful with parents also find ways to foster positive relationships with families in their community. They are positive and welcoming toward parents in the school. These teachers go out of their way to call parents by name and inquire about their children, whether it is in the hallway or at the grocery store. They show their commitment to families by seeking out the parents' opinions, feedback, and ideas regularly. But they also know how to redirect or refocus parents on their shared goal: the social and academic growth of the child. Their reputation becomes one of being fair, honest, open, and confident. This type of teacher is far less likely to be intimidated by challenging parents.

Experienced teachers also learn the skill of disarming a situation by aligning themselves with parents in the best interest of the child. With that focus, the partnership can move forward productively, not blaming each other but working together to find ways to help the child get the best education possible.

A 10-year veteran teacher from a suburban elementary school shares her belief:

> You can move mountains with a positive, supportive, involved, and kind parent partnering with a teacher. When both parties know they are focused on needs and welfare of the child, almost any situation can be handled. I would give anything to have these kinds of relationships, built on mutual trust and respect, in every parent. In the many I've encountered over the years, the children ultimately benefit enormously. They know that their parents and the teacher are a team to support, challenge, encourage, and educate. And that is a powerful thing.

Veteran teachers also seek help with repeatedly challenging parents. They have backup systems, where other teachers support them, should a situation arise. For example, some teachers prefer to meet with chronically difficult parents in pairs, so they feel supported and have someone present to record notes. Other strategies include teachers working in teams (grade-level, special educator, etc.) to back each other up in communications with parents. If teachers are working together to support their students with a clear plan, they will be seen as a unified force that is less likely to be undermined. Other teachers have identified difficult parents and will provide support if they see their fellow teacher in a confrontational discussion with that parent during the school day. Teachers working together in this way can give much-needed support and decrease the feeling of isolation that many teachers experience. Veteran teachers also team with their administrator to have difficult conversations with parents, although this produces varying results depending on the disposition of the administrator.

Another tip of veteran teachers is to save every communication with parents. This way, teachers have a log of interactions they can look back on, or share with someone if necessary. These can be useful years later, especially in the case of an investigation. One teacher saved these files for years, especially when there were cases of suspected abuse toward a child or repeated aggressive communications with school staff. A phone log is another way to document parent communications.

One 30-year veteran teacher described an inspirational parent, who was a tireless advocate not only for her severely disabled son but also for the teachers who worked with him every day:

> Donna had the toughest road you could imagine. Her son had cerebral palsy, and was paralyzed from the neck down. He had no language skills due to the disease, but he was included in the regular fourth-grade classroom as much as possible with the assistance of a one-on-one aide. Donna met frequently with the special education team. She was positive, forward thinking, and efficient. We worked hard as a team to provide the best education for Tim that we were able to. It was not always easy. Donna brought food, her can-do attitude, and ideas to every meeting. I feel Tim was able to participate more fully in his education because Donna could share what worked for him, how we could enrich his experience (without being condescending or having unrealistic expectations). She was a constant advocate, for Tim, for teachers, for education. I will never forget her commitment to her son, and working as part of a team in support of his education.

Together, teachers, parents, school staff, and administration can and should work respectfully, positively, and in a forward-thinking way to meet the needs of the child. As one of the interviewees said, "Then, we can move mountains."

SUCCESS STORIES: PARTNERING TO HELP A CHILD READ AND PARTICIPATE

Parents and teachers working together to help children is a foundation of education, and it is the real, powerful work of education that happens every day. In small and large ways, communication from teachers to parents provides insight into their child's public school education; and likewise, communication from parents to teachers gives a clear picture of the home environment and the wisdom of parents who know their child best. Together, teachers and parents meet to share a child's progress, discuss a problem, make a plan, or change a course of action. When all parties are respectful, open to each other's ideas, and empathetic, the parent-teacher team can unify to enrich, improve, and extend the education of the child.

Take Jack, for example. When he came into Christy's first- and second-grade class, he behaved almost like a feral animal. He would hide under his desk with his things, balled up with fear and anxiety. He came from rural, abject poverty: a house with no heat, filled with rubbish and animals, and barely enough food to get by. And he lived in fear of an abusive family member.

It was no wonder that when he came to first and second grade, schoolwork was the least of his worries. He had to learn basic social skills and feel loved, valued, safe, and fed before he could attend to letters, numbers, and ideas. A very experienced teacher, Christy started making slow but steady progress with Jack each day. And Christy spent a great deal of time talking with Jack's mom, Brenda. Brenda didn't graduate from high school, and didn't have much trust for the school system, based on her own experience with schooling. So it took many communications from Christy before Brenda began to trust her, which happened over the course of the year. As their trust developed, so did their team approach to helping Jack. Jack saw how his mom and teacher talked often, and worked together on helping him with his letters, words, and reading. He knew they both wanted him to be successful, and believed in him. So at school, Jack came out from under the desk and started to look at books and participate in class, but he still sorely lacked social and communication skills. So Christy started plugging Brenda into different community supports and opportunities for Jack (and Brenda's other children). Christy even helped coordinate rides, services, and events so that Jack could attend. Brenda and Jack broke through their isolation from the community, and soon Jack was engaging in regular community activities such as swimming lessons, theatre class, nature walks, and library visits.

Eventually, Jack flourished and learned how to read. His road would never be easy, not with his background, but Jack learned that at least two loving, caring, and committed adults were standing with him. None of this could have happened without the formidable, hardworking, and dedicated teacher-parent team.

THE SILVER LINING: CONTRIBUTING TO A COMMUNITY OVER TIME

While some parent relationships can be adversarial, others develop over time into some of the most significant bonds by which a community can be connected.

Often, the most meaningful tokens of connections to this community are notes written by students or parents; the way a family treats teachers on the street; or how colleagues, parents, and students value teachers' opinions.

Recently, a student named Matt moved from a school where he had been considered a troublemaker, constantly in the principal's office for swearing and fighting. When he moved to his new school, they were warned that he was a "behavior problem" and would need additional support. But Matt didn't have those troubles at his new school. His old school wasn't the right fit for him, and in his new class, he fit beautifully. He succeeded, smiled, and led. After a few months in his class, he learned that he was safe and valued. One day, he gave his teacher a picture he drew of flowers, a sunny day, and animals. It was completely unexpected from this rough and tumble sixth-grade boy. The drawing hangs on the bulletin board behind the teacher's desk, and his teacher loves it dearly.

Meaning and recognition might come when you least expect it. A poem, an essay, a note. Some way that a child or a parent thanks you, references you, or notices what you do every day. When these things happen, they lift us up. There are countless ways teachers affect children and families that we will never know about.

So it's about faith. Believing in what you do, knowing it makes a difference. Keeping your chin up despite what seems like a barrage of things being thrown at you.

Teachers shared about seeing kids in their communities. They loved to see them grow and change, and to see how the children and young adults would say hello and talk about their lives, even years later. This powerful connection to the future, and to the child who came before, is meaningful.

Yes, there is lots of work we can do to make parent and teacher relationships more successful for everyone. But the simple and beautiful truth is that teachers become part of the lives of their students, their families, and the greater community, often in ways they will never know.

ADDITIONAL RESOURCES

Print Resources

Allen, J. (2007). *Creating welcoming schools.* New York: Teacher's College Press.

Epstein, J. (2008). *School, family, and community partnerships* (3rd ed.). Thousand Oaks, CA: Corwin.

Glasgow, N., & Whitney, P. (2009). *What successful schools do to involve families.* Thousand Oaks, CA: Corwin.

Internet Resources

Family and School Partnerships

> Parent Teacher Association (PTA). (n.d.). *Family-school partnerships.* Available from http://pta.org/family_school_partnerships .asp (articles and links)

Parent Guide to School Involvement

> Scholastic. (n.d.). *Parent guide to school involvement.* Available from www2.scholastic.com/browse/collection.jsp?id=70 (links to multiple articles)

Family Involvement Makes a Difference

> Caspe, M., Lopez, M., & Wolos, C. (2006). *Family involvement in elementary school children's education.* Available from www .hfrp.org/publications-resources/browse-our-publications/ family-involvement-in-elementary-school-children-s-education (part of the Harvard Family Research Project)

Family Support America

> Family Support America. (2007). Available from www.family-supportamerica.org

Families as Primary Partners in
Their Child's Development & School Readiness

> Hepburn, K. S. (n.d.). *Families as primary partners in their child's development & school readiness.* Available from www.aecf .org/upload/publicationfiles/families.pdf

Resources to Promote Social and Emotional Health and School

> Knitzer, J., & Lefkowitz, J. (2005, November). *Resources to promote social and emotional health and school readiness in young children and families.* Available from www.nccp.org/publications/ pub_648.html

Only for My Kid: How Privileged Parents Undermine School Reform

> Kohn, A. (1998, April) Only for my kid: How privileged parents undermine school reform. *Phi Delta Kappan.* Available from www.alfiekohn.org/teaching/ofmk.htm

CHAPTER SEVEN

Administrators

Bill was set up from the start. As a new teacher, he was assigned to a class full of students who exhibited behavior problems, learning disabilities, and emotional troubles; Bill's class had it all. And this is common across the United States in hard-to-staff urban and rural schools. Bill was in the inner city teaching fourth grade. One of his very experienced teaching partners had the higher-level students; another team teacher with a few years of experience had the middle-level learners; and Bill had the class full of challenging and difficult behaviors among its students. How can giving a brand-new teacher this class be sustainable, good for students or teachers?

So now, Bill looked out on his new fourth-grade class, and he had no idea how to manage them. His teacher training program didn't prepare him for this. He quit a lucrative publishing job to pursue his master of education degree. He learned about creative, integrated, inquiry-based teaching. His one course in classroom management was all philosophy.

Bill tried everything in the book to get the kids to behave. He tried behavioral charts; used rewards for good behavior; took away time from recess or withheld other privileges as a consequence for inappropriate behavior; called parents; and had other teachers or administrators talk to the class. But nothing worked. Finally he reached out to the assistant principal. That was the beginning of the end for him.

(Continued)

121

(Continued)

When she walked into his classroom, the assistant principal spoke condescendingly to Bill in front of his class, which he believed undermined his authority. She threatened the kids, who were already afraid of her, with punishment for misbehavior, and she took Bill's lessons and taught them while he watched. This kind of modeling could be a good thing, done in a respectful way in an open, positive, and professional relationship. Unfortunately, this was not the case. The kids didn't know who to direct their questions to, and they saw her blatant disrespect for him. He felt small and awful, and the moment she left, the students returned to their terrible behavior.

Bill grew more and more disillusioned and angry. The assistant principal never offered any more support other than to teach his class and show him how "easy" it should be. Bill didn't have a teacher mentor or any established relationships in the school, and he didn't know where to turn. He was alone, confused, and had no idea what to do. His confusion soon turned into depression.

Bill quit teaching in October of his first year. His replacement quit at the end of the school year, as did the principal who hadn't offered him much support. He still runs into parents who tell him he shouldn't have quit, that he had been hired into an impossible situation; but his confidence was so shaken, he says he will never teach again.

It didn't have to be this way for Bill. With a supportive, empathetic, and collaborative principal and a strong teacher mentor, he could have made it through this difficult year. Legions of committed and hardworking administrators help teachers like Bill every day, and many more struggle to find time to offer this kind of support within an already overloaded schedule.

THE PRESSURE COOKER OF THE PRINCIPALSHIP

Today's administrators face an almost impossible job. There are budgets to write, staff to supervise, parents to work with, and communities to please. Principals not only manage school staff and all the students, but they are in charge of the functioning of the entire school—including the physical buildings. Often in the same day, they deal with overflowing toilets, student behavior problems, broken technology, parent complaints, child-abuse reporting, and late school board meetings. And that's just the beginning—in truly troubled inner-city school districts, they might deal with chronic school violence. There is no end to the difficult challenges our nation's administrators face: drug use, teenage pregnancy, child abuse, extreme poverty, and homelessness. Administrators are pulled in countless directions. Some principals handle this role with impressive professionalism, empathy, and support. Others, not so well. Even the best of principals sometimes react negatively to the pressures they face.

PRESSURE FROM PARENTS

Some of the pressing issues administrators must deal with are the concerns of vocal parents, many of whom come to them with complaints about staff. Often, the principal is put in the difficult position of acting as a mediator between the teacher and parent. Sometimes, the parent is given credibility before the principal hears the story and impressions of the teacher. Then, the principal knows only part of the story. When the principal approaches the teacher, the teacher is likely to feel defensive.

"One of the most frustrating things about teaching," said eight-year teaching veteran Donald, "is when a parent circumvents direct communication with me and instead goes to the principal. Countless times, when I have been teaching, a parent will come to the door and want to speak with me at that particular moment. I am usually engaged in the act of teaching and can't do this. Frustrated, the parent heads for the principal instead. The principal then listens to a tirade that should have been handled at the classroom level, and now they are involved. Their perceptions of the teacher can change based on these interactions, and that is not fair. Parents need to come directly to teachers, and if we are teaching, they need to call, send an e-mail, or set up a meeting."

An elementary teacher in a small, rural school spoke of how certain parents teamed with administrators to micromanage assignments, rubrics, and instructional methods. If the parent is a school board member, the pressure and expectation grows immensely. These parents are often given more opportunities, more time, and more accommodations than any other parents. And the constantly moving target—the shifting, parent-identified goals, which may be driven by what is best for their child and not necessarily what is best for other students—can be frustrating for teachers who are always under the microscope.

Sometimes, the problem is simply lack of experience. Administrators who haven't spent much time teaching have very little understanding of current-day classrooms. If they haven't been in the field for a number of years, or didn't teach much to begin with, administrators may not understand how much time the job actually takes to do well.

Stacy, a teacher in an affluent suburban middle school, explains that her principal would "throw her under the bus" with parents at any time. She's learned by experience that her administrator will take the students' or the parents' perspective more seriously than her own. So she works in isolation. She does her job as best as she can, never asking for help or support and never collaborating and problem solving with her principal. She said, "Now I shut my door, and pray to God no one complains." What kind of learning environment is this? How sustainable is a model of isolation for teachers? Unfortunately, many teachers in this situation will adopt a plan similar to Stacy's: "[The principal] is driving good teachers away from this school. I'm giving it this year, and then I am getting out."

TESTING PRESSURE

Today, administrators are under constant pressure to improve test scores every year from parents, superintendents, and local and national officials. This pressure is then, in many cases, transferred squarely onto the shoulders of educators.

Take Jen, for example. She works in an affluent intermediate school and explains how her entire teaching day is scripted and focused on improving test scores. This school uses a guided basal reading program and a structured math program. The principal requires that they follow these programs exactly, regardless of student ability or interest. The staff are not allowed to deviate from the teacher guide. In her school, they have a reading specialist who comes around to check what page of the book the teachers are on. The teachers need to be on the same page, literally, every day; despite the fact that they have different students with different needs, abilities, and backgrounds.

The students take five tests each week, and that is only in reading. This is all in preparation for the end-of-the-year tests. "These kids have at least one test every single day. No wonder they act out! They have no creativity left. They are master test takers, but they can't think," said Jen. And teachers are publicly judged by their students' test scores in a meeting led by their principal. Scores are projected onto a huge screen and what happened with each class is discussed, with the whole staff. Now, this could be done respectfully in a school where everyone trusts one another and works toward improving student learning as a community. But not at this school. So once teachers know they will be openly criticized in this environment, what do they do? All they talk about is test scores. They are in what Jen calls "terror mode." A feeling of competition grows among teachers, so no one wants to share ideas or collaborate. Everyone wonders: What if I don't make it, what am I going to do?

We know from current teacher literature, such as *Professional Learning Communities at Work* (Dufour & Eaker, 1998), that teacher isolation is a major stumbling block to developing professional learning communities (where educators "create an environment that fosters mutual cooperation, emotional support, and personal growth as they work together to achieve what they cannot accomplish alone," p. xii). And this sense of isolation is one of the greatest sources of job dissatisfaction for teachers. A climate such as the one experienced by Bill or Stacy or Jen is exactly the kind of isolating, test-focused environment that alienates the staff and can, ultimately, drive them from the classroom.

TIME PRESSURE

Personal Days

Megan was horrified when she asked her principal for a personal day—and he asked her what it was for. She hadn't anticipated that question, because she thought her personal day was, well, personal. What she didn't realize was that many districts still have a line or two in their contracts about what teachers can and can't do on their personal time. Teachers get between three and five personal days a year. These are the only times during the school year when teachers can elect to take a day off. Some principals, though, use guilt and pressure (or even directives) to lessen, change, or dictate these days.

In Megan's case, her principal researched how many days she had used—and who in the district hadn't used any personal days at all. Then, when he asked her what her personal day was for, he added that many teachers don't take their personal days, and he proceeded to name a few from the district. The implicit message: They are better, more dedicated, and more selfless teachers than you are. The irony is that she wanted to use her personal time to write her report cards, which she didn't have enough class time to do because she was mentoring a new teacher.

The principal said to Megan, "Your students need you," when she requested a personal day. Well, of course they do! But don't they also need a respected professional, who has time to visit family, renew her driver's license, or do whatever the rest of the country does on their days off? Some administrators know that teachers will react to this pressure and feel guilty about taking their earned personal time—or not take it at all. What financial advisor in the world would tell you to forgo three paid days? Like all professionals, teachers are entitled to their days off.

Committee Meetings

Administrators can also exert pressure on teachers to work on school or district committees. Working on committees isn't usually required by contract (or if it is, the contract usually sets a certain number of hours). But teachers are often pressured to serve on committees—more than can fit into this allotted time.

Through e-mails, notes in staff mailboxes, direct inquiries, and in some cases, directives from the principals (or curriculum coordinators), teachers can be pressured into taking on too many committee responsibilities. In one school where I conducted interviews, the classroom teachers were there hours before school started, almost every day of the week, attending various committee meetings. There was no one keeping track of the committees, who was on them or how their synergistic effect might impact one's planning and teaching. The stress in the building was palpable as teachers rushed to various meetings instead of preparing for the day's lessons.

What ends up happening in most committees? Some work. Lots and lots of talking. And a good deal of complaining—mostly, about the same problems that have been going on for years. There are very few products or positive results for students that come out of large committees with time-crunched teachers. During the meetings, I would bet most teachers are thinking about their day and how to best teach their students. The issue of unproductive committees is discussed in Hal Portner's 2008 article, "Committees: Make Them More Productive." He suggests several ideas to make committees more productive for everyone, such as making them action oriented and respectful to everyone involved.

Committee meetings make life especially hard for teachers who have families. Early and late committee meetings impact child-care costs, family relationships, and healthy behaviors. Most of these teachers end up prepping for their classes and grading papers at night, after their children are in bed. This is often in place of exercise, communicating with family, or just plain relaxing: all activities which help to prevent burnout.

In many of the schools I surveyed, a few teachers end up taking on most of the committee responsibilities. This may be out of guilt or a sense of responsibility, or feeling that their own family responsibilities are not as great as others. While this is noble and kind, it is not healthy for these professionals.

Teachers know they must work together to solve problems, improve curricula, and make positive changes in their schools. By focusing on one or two committee responsibilities, teachers can give more fully of their time and energy to forward school initiatives. Administrators can be a positive force by leading the staff to select critical committees for the year and by balancing the responsibilities among the staff based on equity and interest.

Disciplinary Pressure

Many teachers have challenging students, ones for whom the regular discipline system does not work well. These students disrupt the learning for the rest of the class, in some cases daily. When teachers cry for help, some administrators have no idea how to help the situation and end up simply sending the disruptive student back into class, without a plan or system in place for improvement.

This was the case for a middle school teacher, Juan. One of his students would come into class "swearing at me, turning over desks, throwing books," day after day. When one student demands complete attention, the teacher is not available for quality instruction. And when classmates are scared, they are not available for learning. The student did not care about consequences; and the teachers, guidance counselors, and administrators were unsuccessful in coming up with an alternate plan. Juan repeatedly asked for help, but his administrators were overwhelmed and were not able to lend support. This perpetuated a vicious cycle: The student would act out, be sent from class, and come back—and now, frustrated by not knowing what was going on in class, would act out again. This continued for most of the school year. Then, the pupil was retained and, presumably, the pattern of disruption continued. The child was a good candidate for behavior intervention: a functional behavior assessment, a behavior specialist, a behavior plan, and perhaps social-skill instruction and counseling. This youth may have benefited from an evaluation or an alternative program. We'll never know. The damage was done. The child floundered in school, the other students in class lost out on their education, and Juan quit teaching after a few short years.

Fifth-grade teacher Liza, working in an inner-city school, describes a similar situation as her greatest frustration in teaching:

> The most challenging situation that I have been in was when we were told that any student with behavior issues and who is disrupting the class, we need to deal with it and not have them out of the class. One of my classes loses about 20–30 minutes a day due to behavior issues, and the students are not getting the attention and education that they need, due to disruptive students. I am trying to manage the student's disruptive behavior, teach the rest of the class, and keep everyone on task while differentiating the lessons so my students that are on a second-grade reading level do not fall behind. In turn, if a student fails, we are questioned (1) why and (2) what are you doing to help this student?

In such challenging situations, involving students for whom regular disciplinary consequences don't work, teachers need a creative problem-solving approach and a strong administrator who can help make tough decisions to support everyone involved. What teachers don't need is to be told to deal with it themselves, while every other student in the class loses valuable education time.

Many times, teachers feel the administrators are neither supportive nor strict enough when it comes to discipline. No one wants to go back to the days of corporal punishment, but an expectation for respectful behavior from students seems to be dwindling. One middle school science teacher was among those who described various situations in which they were dismayed by a lack of consequences for unacceptable behavior:

> A student in my class called another a racial slur. I sent him out of the class to the principal, and he was back later that afternoon to attend a field trip. I was dismayed that he was able to join our field trip without any processing or discussion from the administrator with me or with the affected student. My students learned quickly that consequences for bad behavior are light and fleeting. It's no wonder I have constant behavior problems.

MENTORS HELP PRINCIPALS, TOO

In all the directions that principals are pulled, it only seems right that they are given support to help them with their ever-changing and challenging positions. Quality induction programs for teachers have proved to be successful, according to an article about teacher attrition in the *Review of Educational Research* (Borman & Dowling, 2008), so why aren't there more opportunities for administrators to have mentors?

According to Betsy, a suburban primary school special educator, administrators must be knowledgeable:

> Schools need experienced, well-trained administrators who have respectful personalities. Administrators need to be able to interact well with others, consider change thoughtfully, make

decisions, encourage staff, and be able to say "no" to parents or staff, when needed. There is no comparison between an administrator who has years of teaching experience versus an administrator with limited or no classroom experience. To better support their staff and understand grade level demands and curriculum, effective administrators must have experience and knowledge at the level they are supervising. They must understand the realities of being in the classroom day-to-day.

I have seen new administrators also greatly benefit from mentoring programs where recently retired principals help those new to the field. We need to reduce administrator turnover by supporting them, too.

By having a weekly meeting with a retired or fellow administrator, principals can share strategies, bounce ideas off each other, and problem solve challenging issues and situations. These meetings can be a lifeline in an overwhelmed administrator's schedule and can help the principal develop more positive relationships with teachers, students, and parents.

RECOMMENDATIONS FOR ADMINISTRATORS AND TEACHER LEADERS

• Advocate for a paid, organized mentor system to be set up for administrators.

• Establish communication protocols for parents, encouraging them to make an appointment with the teacher and talk with them first about any concern. Principals should ask, "Have you spoken to your child's teacher about this yet?" before getting into any discussions about any perceived problems or issues.

• Consider all perspectives. Ask teachers about the background, educational reasoning, and goals of a decision they've made, before making any judgments. Seek to understand the issue from both the parent's and the teacher's points of view.

• Listen to and collaborate with teachers to problem solve, rather than seeking to affix blame.

- Recognize that standardized testing is not the ultimate goal of education. Encourage teacher growth through professional development (during schooltime or for graduate credit), dialogue, and other supportive techniques. Be aware that encouraging competition among teachers will only alienate them from each other.

- Support teachers with difficult, challenging students. Work with guidance counselors, behavioral specialists, and special educators to develop creative ideas and team approaches for how to help disruptive students so they and other students can learn. Attend workshops with teachers about how to manage challenging behaviors.

- Implement a consistent, schoolwide behavior plan for all classrooms.

Example: Rumney Memorial School's Discipline Procedure

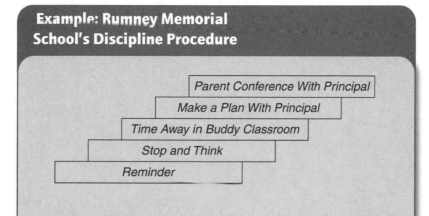

Parent Conference With Principal

Make a Plan With Principal

Time Away in Buddy Classroom

Stop and Think

Reminder

Discipline at Rumney is based on helping students take control of their actions so that all students are able to learn. There is a progression of disciplinary actions and procedures. Consistent application of the procedures outlined is critical to the success of the approach.

Steps in Our Discipline Procedure

Reminder(s): Reminders are given to students who are not meeting school behavior expectations. Example: A student having a side conversation during class will be given a reminder to stop talking and to pay attention to the lesson.

(Continued)

(Continued)

Stop and Think: If a reminder is not sufficient, and a student's disruptive behavior continues, the student needs to be removed to an area in the classroom to take a break or a time out. The student is asked to return to the group when he/she feels ready to rejoin the lesson. Example: A student continues to have a side conversation after the reminder, so he or she will be asked to take a break.

Time Away in Buddy Classroom: Another kind of break is a visit to the "Buddy Classroom." This is another classroom where the student can take a short break. Each classroom has a designated buddy classroom, and students do not spend more than five minutes during this time away. Example: Any behavior which continues after a reminder and Stop and Think—this could be a side conversation or other disruptions. Students know that the next step after the Buddy Classroom is to make a plan with the principal.

Make a Plan With Principal: Students are asked to make plans after three classroom interventions have not succeeded. The purpose of this is to help the student develop a plan to stop the negative behavior. A student will be asked to explain what the behavior was and how it affected others. He or she will then be asked to develop a plan to stop this behavior. A copy of this plan will be sent home, parents are asked to sign and return one copy, and keep a copy for themselves. A sample planning sheet is on the following page. Teachers will refer to this plan and use it to help students control their behavior.

Parent Conference With Principal: Parent conferences can occur when making a plan is not solving the problem, or when the behavior escalates to an extreme level or compromises the safety of students in the school. The principal and the classroom teacher will meet with the student and parents to decide what further actions need to be taken to stop the disruptive behavior.

↗*Fast Track:* Our discipline plan is designed to preserve the safety and integrity of the school and class communities. If at any time an adult in the building feels that the safety or integrity of a student, class, or the school is at risk due to a student's behavior, that student will immediately be sent to the principal for further action.

Source: Rumney Memorial School (2008a).

WORDS OF WISDOM FROM VETERAN TEACHERS

Veteran teachers encourage teachers from all levels to be involved in the hiring of administrators. Ask the tough questions. Read the recommendations. Talk with their current coworkers. Visit their old school. Pick the person with the most teaching experience, and the most understanding of the issues facing teachers in public schools today.

In tough behavior situations, with a lack of support from administrators, a beginning teacher described her way to make sense of her world:

> In order for me to keep sane, I re-assess the situation and make sure that I did everything I could and if the student(s) fail, I know that I did my best. We also have a small support group and we meet once a week and that helps a lot. I also tell myself that I can't save every student but if I make a difference in at least one . . . I did my job and it keeps me going.

This sort of positive self talk and support is essential to helping teachers work within a system that is overwhelming.

Another way to improve the quality of communication between teachers and administrators is to advocate for the school to provide mentors for new administrators. The school community can advocate for hiring a seasoned principal to meet weekly, or as needed, with newer principals to share ideas, discuss problems, and provide leadership. This way, the principal has a sounding board and can process and practice difficult conversations and situations before they happen. This mentor should be available for at least the first year, preferably two.

Brian, a fourth-grade elementary teacher sums it up when he describes the necessary characteristics for principals:

> It takes an experienced, courageous, charismatic, levelheaded, confident, intelligent, innate manager to lead a public school, especially these days with the push for perfection, high test scores, differentiation to all levels of learners and all speakers of all languages. It is a job only for those with the best of management and interpersonal skills, and for those that have true empathy for teachers in today's classroom setting.

🏆 SUCCESS STORIES: PRINCIPAL MENTORS MAKE A DIFFERENCE

Fortunately, some school districts recognize that being a principal can be isolating, overwhelming, and stressful. Principal mentors can provide guidance, support, and the wisdom of years of experience to aid new principals in their leadership positions. Administrators are at great risk for attrition and burnout, and there are models for principal mentorship that can have powerful impacts on school leadership.

The Savannah-Chatham School District in Georgia began its principal mentoring program in 2007, wanting to lessen principal attrition and provide critical support for their school leaders. According to an *Education World* (Delisio, 2007) story about the program, "Mentors may guide, instruct, watch, or just listen. Several new principals said having that reassuring presence or voice on the phone is making all the difference as they start their careers as administrators" (para. 5). Mentors make themselves available for weekly meetings, telephone calls, and e-mail communication as needed.

This mentoring powerfully affects new principals as they navigate the challenges of the job. James Heater (Delisio, 2007), a first-year principal said, "You don't know exactly what's expected of you until you are in the position; there is no way to comprehend how busy and how many decisions you make in a second. My mentor has done it—she can give me hints and tips" (para. 15).

This district is recognizing the varied and increasing challenges facing administrators and is putting in place a program to assist them. This benefits everyone: the students, the teachers, and the school community. Veteran administrators share their real-life skills, experiences, and procedures with new principals trying to figure it all out in isolation. As educators, we talk about a model of collaboration for veteran and new teachers in the form of comprehensive teacher-induction programs. It is just as important to avoid isolation and burnout for our nation's administrators.

These mentors should be paid, in recognition of the professional responsibility they are being asked to fulfill. Albuquerque, New Mexico, provides a stipend to its principal mentors, and uses an online forum where new principals can ask questions and seek advice from veteran administrators. This proved invaluable to one principal, Barbara Martin (Curtis, 2002), who said, "I had a great first year. . . . I chalk that up to the advice I had online, and I had great mentors here [in the school district]. . . . You don't need to reinvent the wheel if you can learn from other people's mistakes" (para. 13).

Together, we can learn from each other. Schools should create support systems for teachers and administrators, to help them with the growing challenges they face on a daily basis.

ADDITIONAL RESOURCES

Print Resources

Blase, J., & Blase, J. (2002). *Breaking the silence: Overcoming the problem of principal mistreatment of teachers.* Thousand Oaks, CA: Corwin.

Capasso, R. L., & Daresh, J. C. (2001). *The school administrator internship handbook: Leading, mentoring, and participating in the internship program.* Thousand Oaks, CA: Corwin.

Lindley, F. (2008). *The portable mentor: A resource guide for entry-year principals and mentors.* Thousand Oaks, CA: Corwin.

Pawlas, G. (2005). *The administrator's guide to school-community relations.* Larchmont, NY: Eye on Education.

Schmidt, L. (2002). *Gardening in the minefield: A survival guide for school administrators.* Portsmouth, NH: Heinemann.

Whitaker, T. (2003). *What great principals do differently: 15 things that matter most.* Larchmont, NY: Eye on Education.

Wilmore, E. (2004). *Principal induction: A standards-based model for administrator development.* Thousand Oaks, CA: Corwin.

Internet Resources

Principal Mentorship Examples, Articles, and Links

Malone, J. (2001/2002, Winter). Principal mentoring: An update. *Research Roundup.* Available from http://cepm.uoregon .edu/publications/roundup/Winter_01-02.html

New York City Principal Leadership Academy

Wallace Foundation. (n.d.). *NYC leadership guide: Training effective principals* [Video file]. Available from www.wallacefoundation .org/principal-story/vignettes-and-conversation-guides/Pages/ nyc-leadership-academy.aspx

Characteristics of Successful Mentoring Programs

Holloway, J. (2004, April). Mentoring new leaders. *Educational Leadership*. Available from http://ascd.org/publications/edu cational_leadership/apr04/vol61/num07/_Mentoring_New _Leaders.aspx

Changing Role of School Leadership

National Education Association. (2008). *Changing role of school leadership*. Available from www.nea.org/assets/docs/mf_ PB09_Leadership.pdf (an article with an overview of the changing landscape of principal leadership)

CHAPTER EIGHT

School Boards

Megan and Jennifer came to the school board meeting at their little rural elementary school at 6:30 pm. They wanted to discuss the current report card and how it wasn't good educational practice to report both grades and standards on the same card. Everything they'd read said that this practice undermined the use of standards and made calculating grades different for every teacher. As the only two teachers for their grade level, they often had different letter grades (A through F) for students who had the same numbers for standards (1 through 4).

So after teaching all day, they waited for their turn to speak to the school board. Megan was nervous as she watched how the school board interacted. They were fiery and testy with one another on small issues they were discussing. She wondered how they would react to this one. In the district only a few years, she didn't want to ruffle any feathers. She also knew that the report card had to be reviewed, and hopefully changed, if they were to use a standards-based report card. She breathed in deeply, trying to relax until it was their turn.

An hour later, Megan rubbed her eyes. It was getting late. Finally, they were called on to start the discussion, and Megan passed out the report card information. Immediately, the board members chimed in, commenting that grades are important, that they had grades as children, and that parents like them. Megan tried to direct them to the research section of the handout; she explained the reasoning behind the idea to move to a standards-based report card, to no avail. The board members were busy interrupting each other and touting the

(Continued)

(Continued)

importance of grades, without hearing the well-developed reasoning from the two educational experts in the room with master's degrees. Megan tried to get a word in edgewise, then gave up. Jennifer looked pale; she didn't say a word. Then the board moved on to other topics, and the teachers left: frustrated, defeated, and wondering why their voices were never heard.

SHARED LEADERSHIP

There is no doubt that most school board members are committed public servants who want what is best for students. They volunteer countless hours to improve our nation's schools, bringing a local connection and commitment to the job. School boards meet for hours well into the evening to shape the school's budget; discussing building maintenance, supply budgets, heating systems, and curricular expenses with great attention to detail. School boards make many hard decisions about how to manage our schools, often taking on controversial and challenging situations. The school board's job is complex: They might manage the school's finances, oversee hiring and personnel issues, make important schoolwide decisions about programs, and work closely with the principal, teachers, and parents to continually improve the school. The nature and extent of their duties vary from state to state, with some school boards overseeing small individual schools, and others overseeing whole districts with many schools.

The decisions that school boards make are critical. When these decisions involve curriculum, assessment, or educational programs, and the school board members have no background in education or current educational practices, they might not be the individuals best suited to make them. And our current system may not be the best way to make use of this valuable resource.

A high school English teacher echoed these concerns:

I think teachers need to be listened to more seriously. We are experts in our field who are forced to defer to nonexperts, who sometimes sit on a very high horse. This can be frustrating and demoralizing. If I were to go in for an appendectomy and find out it was being planned and executed by a bunch of amateurs who were all in on the operation because they expected some political gain . . . I'd probably just try to remove my appendix myself. The political maneuverings that take place on school boards, that are supposed to be charged with orchestrating the educational system here, are simply offensive. There is not a single teacher sitting on a committee that's supposed to be in charge of education. It just makes me scratch my head.

This teacher's remarks highlight the problem of school board members who volunteer because they have a particular axe to grind with public education or because they want to use the position as a springboard for other political opportunities.

An elementary teacher noticed how school boards have a great impact on passing school budgets, sometimes with little understanding of the curriculum and how the school functions:

I find it absurd that people with no educational training or experience run the school boards. These board members do not understand or even know what the curriculum is. I know because my principal has started scheduling teachers to attend the evening board meetings to make presentations to the board about our programs and what we teach. I feel certain our board members couldn't tell me one standard if I put them on the spot; yet they make all of the major decisions for the school. Each board micromanages their local school, with the typical board member there to push some issue related to their individual child. Then the community votes every year on the school budget, again primarily relying on people with no educational training and very limited education experience. These are the same people who do not want to pay higher taxes. It is a challenge every year to get the budget passed (with increases typically hovering only at the rate of inflation). If the budget gets voted down, cuts are made and a revote is held. I say all of this knowing that our school is one of the highest performing, most respected schools in the area; yet funding for it is no guarantee.

There can be a dramatic conflict of interest when school board members have children in the school. The conversation and actions of the board can then shift from a larger schoolwide set of goals, to micromanaging a classroom around a specific issue related to the child of a school board member. Many school board members with children in the school manage this well and professionally, but not all. And when the micromanaging comes down to the educational decisions based at the classroom level, concerning projects and assignments, according to some teachers, it can feel particularly meddlesome and disrespectful.

A third-grade teacher with six years of experience illustrated this point:

> When board members are discussing classroom assignments and issues at board meetings, they are also setting up a negative tone for future parents in higher grade levels. Also, the bigger, schoolwide issues (of which there are always many) are not being discussed. The classroom issues should be discussed with the teacher at a scheduled meeting. Many times, the school board is discussing an assignment or classroom practice they don't know anything about, and the teacher isn't there to explain it. And yet they are making decisions about classroom issues anyway.

School boards are a wonderful example of community involvement, investment, and leadership in a school; and like everything in education, their role may need to evolve in ways that build stronger relationships and trust within the school community. Ways to do this are explored in Recommendations for Administrators and Teacher Leaders.

USES AND ABUSES OF POWER

There are legions of committed, respectful, kind, and hardworking school board members across our country. But in a few of the schools where I have interviewed teachers, school board members have used their position to exert power within the school, sometimes unknowingly.

In one elementary school where I interviewed several teachers, there was a group of teachers and school board members who would gossip about other teachers and students. That group started to become a powerful clique in the school community, and many teachers started to feel uncomfortable; those who avoided the clique were targeted for their various positions and practices. The board members and a few teachers would talk about other teachers and the principal negatively, often in the hallway. The climate of the school changed completely, and everyone became fearful and mistrusting.

School board members can also wield power in a school by having the ear and the attention of the principal. In another school where I interviewed teachers, school board members would hang out for hours in the office, talking with the principal or the office staff; much of the talk involved classroom issues that should have been handled with the teacher. In such cases, board members were then privy to the many issues and situations the principal and the office were handling. Or they'd have conversations in the hallways with other parents about confidential issues or their child's teacher. Teachers became very uncomfortable moving through the halls of their own schools, hearing conversations quiet when they walk by. Often, these conversations yielded the kind of call that all teachers dread. A parent would say, "Several parents feel that this issue is a problem," making clear to the teacher that one parent began a griping campaign, and enlisted others to join in, to gang up and get what they want. This approach to a problem does not foster a feeling of community and teambuilding among parents and teachers.

One teacher I interviewed described seeing several school board members who would linger in front of or inside the school for hours, talking about classroom concerns and school issues. Often, these members would team up to demand a change in a class project, activity, or program—usually about an issue that involved their own children. "When I would see these two talking outside," said Susie, an elementary school math and science teacher, "I could feel my blood pressure rising. I knew I would have an e-mail from one or both of these parents, making some small or large demand."

Sarah, another elementary school teacher, described being bullied by a school board member on regular occasions. He would seek her out, often in the middle of the day while she was teaching, and make demands on behalf of his son, who was in her class. Every time she saw him in the building, she became stressed out and worried:

> He would talk in circles, making statements about his son's education that weren't true. I'd defend my teaching and my program fully, and then he would circle back again to his

perceived problem, changing it only slightly and becoming more agitated. He would speak condescendingly to me in front of other staff and in front of students. Often what he was saying was entirely untrue. And he was a school board member! He would take his misinformation and spite for my teaching with him to every school board meeting. When we hired a new principal, I worried that this school board member would tarnish my reputation before the principal even met me or saw me teach.

Some school board members are not respectful of privacy issues. In one middle school, a teacher was asked about her teaching partner's marital problems and her plans for the following year. Such questions, which have no impact on teaching, are out of bounds and put teachers in a difficult position. The teacher who wants to develop a strong working relationship with board members can either answer them—and then feel badly because they participated in gossip and overstepped a professional boundary—or they can say they aren't comfortable answering, which leads to an awkward conversation. The choices are tough.

One former elementary school board member commented on the situation:

There is not much other school board members can do about inappropriate lines of conversation or behavior from another school board member. The board can publicly censure another board member if they are acting outrageously, but otherwise, there is really nothing the board can do. It is what it is, and a school board member can ride out their term.

you can... DO IT! RECOMMENDATIONS FOR ADMINISTRATORS AND TEACHER LEADERS

• First and foremost, set up a schoolwide culture of respect. This is essential and is the responsibility of the entire school community. School board members must know that everyone in the building is respected on an equal level. Hallway gossip, belittling or disrespecting teachers (or board members), should not be tolerated. A tone of partnership and teaming for the success of each student and for the welfare of the school community should be paramount.

- If negative hallway conversations or teacher bullying and power wielding happen, the administrator can meet with the school board to discuss how damaging this could be, both to individual teachers and to the positive functioning of the school. Or a team of teachers and the administration can come to a board meeting to discuss the issue.

- Employ a "Have you talked to your child's classroom teacher about this first?" rule with school board members. Because school board members work so closely with the principal, they talk with him or her often and may take a question or an issue to the principal instead of the teacher. This can cause myriad problems. By asking that simple question first, much strife can be avoided.

- Solicit more feedback from educators. One way to do this is to set up a teacher advisory council that assists the school board. Two teachers from the school could have a yearly commitment to attend all school board meetings and offer educational expertise, institutional memory (a working knowledge of the past practices, community history, and the curricular past of a school), and the teacher perspective to the school board. This would be more powerful if teachers were equal players, their input valued and used in decision making. Teachers on this council could receive a small stipend similar to the amount each school board member receives (funding could be added to the budget and approved by the community). Other schools have created a leadership model that includes a team of parents, teachers, school staff, and sometimes students (in middle and high school). See Success Stories for an example of this.

- Recruit teams of teachers to partner with the school board during the school year. Teachers in this case could attend meetings to provide insight and to report back to the appropriate staff any important information. This is a first step that could be somewhat manageable for teachers to begin right away.

- Work with school staff and the school board to create a school board code of ethics, or adopt the code endorsed by the National School Boards Association (NSBA), and commit to upholding it (see Code of Ethics for School Board Members).

Code of Ethics for School Board Members Endorsed by the NSBA

As a member of my local Board of Education I will strive to improve public education, and to that end I will

- attend all regularly scheduled board meetings insofar as possible, and become informed concerning the issues to be considered at those meetings;
- recognize that I should endeavor to make policy decisions only after full discussion at publicly held board meetings;
- render all decisions based on the available facts and my independent judgment, and refuse to surrender that judgment to individuals or special interest groups;
- encourage the free expression of opinion by all board members, and seek systematic communications between the board and students, staff, and all elements of the community;
- work with other board members to establish effective board policies and to delegate authority for the administration of the schools to the superintendent;
- communicate to other board members and the superintendent expression of public reaction to board policies and school programs;
- inform myself about current educational issues by individual study and through participation in programs providing needed information, such as those sponsored by my state and national school boards association;
- support the employment of those persons best qualified to serve as school staff, and insist on a regular and impartial evaluation of all staff;
- avoid being placed in a position of conflict of interest;
- take no private action that will compromise the board or administration, and respect the confidentiality of information that is privileged under applicable law; and
- remember always that my first and greatest concern must be the educational welfare of the students attending the public schools.

Source: National School Boards Association (1999).

- Establish some sort of support system for the teacher to be put into effect when difficult situations between teachers and school board members arise. This support could be a guidance counselor who suggests strategies for good communication and mediates a meeting, or another individual or group a teacher can call on to help mediate.

- Develop a protocol that teachers review at the beginning of the year, to be used in the event that a school board member is bullying an educator. This could involve steps such as documentation, team meetings, and finally, some sort of grievance letter to be sent to the school board or to the superintendent.

- Use the same communication protocols for school board members that are set up for all parents at the beginning of the school year.

- Be active and aware, know your teachers, and communicate what is happening in your school to the school board.

- Seek input from teachers about what they are currently doing before discussing criticisms with school board members.

- Encourage school board members to spend a day substitute teaching in classrooms. This way, they can begin to understand perspectives of teachers.

- Discuss with the school board what matters are open for school board discussion, and which are within the jurisdiction of the certified, trained educator in the classroom. That way, the school board and administrator can redirect conversations as needed.

- Encourage, or even work with the superintendent to require, school board members to attend training about how to be effective in supporting the school. Trainings are regularly offered in most states.

 ## WORDS OF WISDOM
FROM VETERAN TEACHERS

While looking back at my interviews and thinking about my experiences, I realized there was not much information about how to deal with challenging school board members. This is telling. Teachers are confounded about how to deal with difficult, power-wielding school board members. After all, these are likely the people who hired them. Powerful school board members can contribute to a stressful, threatening climate and, ultimately, drive educators out of the classroom.

Despite this, many experienced teachers see school board members as their allies in the work of education. Veteran teachers explain themselves fully, they demonstrate the good work they are doing, and they are not threatened by differing opinions or misunderstandings, as long as they are handled respectfully.

I've seen veteran teachers be polite but direct when communicating with a school board member who is attempting to micromanage. Also, teachers have developed tactics for situations where they might be cornered by a school board member and feel uncomfortable. Sometimes they meet with another teacher present, or they plan to have another teacher walk in to check on the conversation.

One thing experienced teachers learn is that sometimes they have to be their own public-relations specialists, promoting the good work they are doing. Even though this is difficult in an already packed schedule, certain years with certain parents call for this.

SUCCESS STORIES: SCHOOL BOARD, ADMINISTRATOR, AND TEACHER TEAMS

At the Local Level: At the prekindergarten screening in one community, it became apparent that there were lots of three- and four-year-olds and not enough prekindergarten slots to school all of them. This caused great worry and discussion among parents, who had grown to love and expect a prekindergarten option for their young children. When teachers noticed this problem, the principal and school board members began working together to find a solution that best served this population of early learners and their families.

In a collaborative team, the school board, principal, prekindergarten teachers, and classroom assistants worked together to identify several options. Then, they solicited feedback from parents. One school board member described the process:

Instead of jumping to fix this problem without much thought, we really did a good job, taking our time and gathering information. We worked closely with the prekindergarten teachers, parents, the public, we gathered feedback, and set a tone that opened up dialogue. It could've been a heated, passionate debate, but it was disarming that there was no pressure to make a decision right then. We were just gathering information. In this decision-making process, we listened, worked closely with teachers, and made a decision that we felt was best for the community.

This is when boards are at their best: working together with teachers, community members, parents, and the principal to solve schoolwide problems and issues.

One former principal, who was also a board member, discussed an ideal school board member and the requirements for being on a school board.

You have to be willing to put in the time. It is a significant commitment. You need to be knowledgeable about so many issues and have a willingness to be proficient in areas that may or may not be of interest to you. Being a school board member is to be put in a position of trust. You have to feel comfortable enough to make those decisions. Above all, you have to always remember your goal to serve the children and community's best interests. If you have any personal or political intentions that detract from this, you shouldn't be on the board.

At the State Level: One state worked out a unique way to get more input from teachers in their leadership model. The Florida Department of Education set up school advisory councils, or SAC. The members of the SAC comprise parents, teachers, community leaders, school staff, and administrators. These councils provide assistance to school boards, which allows teachers to have increased input on policy making. The group is charged with the important responsibility of making decisions about many school issues, including developing teacher professionalism, improving student performance, assisting with creating budgets, and school reorganizing and restructuring. As a *Phi Delta Kappan* (Kumar, 2000) article described, advisory councils give their members an increased responsibility and voice in the policy-making process:

> By directly involving teachers in school restructuring, SAC enhances quality of instruction and assures successful implementation of policy decisions affecting building—as well as districtwide reform in education. Teacher members of SAC have a unique opportunity to impact policy decisions in the areas of curriculum, management, and evaluation. Their roles in defining goals and plans for technology implementation in school are also significant. SAC is an example of teacher involvement in policy decisions that should be examined by other educational systems as a significant opportunity for education reform. (para. 14)

Whether it is at a local level or statewide, teacher involvement in school and districtwide policy decisions will improve our schools, educational climate, and communities.

THE SILVER LINING: BUOYED BY A SUPPORTIVE COMMUNITY

There's no doubt that the staff of a school can make every day a little brighter and easier, or it can send teachers looking for other opportunities in a matter of months. When a teacher finds a mentor or supportive colleagues, they can be a life raft in a churning sea of testing, state mandates, and challenging students, parents, or school board members.

In some cases, it may be a small group of teachers, and in small schools, it may be most of the staff, but the adults in schools make a huge difference in the overall climate. How can a supportive staff lift up fellow teachers?

Samantha, a special educator, knows:

> I also feel tremendous support from the positive and forward-thinking staff with whom I work. Their open-minded, thoughtful approach sustains me. They respectfully stand up for what they believe, yet they are not afraid to make changes when it makes sense. The principal sets the

tone and expectations for the building. But day to day, it is the staff who maintain it. The staff at my school are particularly caring and thoughtful; they look out for one another. When someone is really sick, there are kind notes, a thoughtful meal or two, or even just a simple exchange asking how the person is doing. There is an underlying current of caring for one another. Our school staff donate a little money each year to a fund where two staff members take the initiative (on behalf of all of us) to support staff who experience loss, sadness, or extreme stress. The gestures are simple, but thoughtful . . . a card, flowers, dinner. They make a difference. It cultivates a caring community.

These small gestures do make a difference in the daily lives of teachers. By looking out for each other and not living in isolation, teachers can rely on each other in meaningful ways. They can go to each other for help with issues with students, administrators, and parents. Having a team of people ready to help you talk through an issue is invaluable. That is why it is so important for new teachers to have a comprehensive induction program, not just a single mentor they meet with infrequently. Teachers need a family of educators standing with them to sustain the challenges they face.

Christine described a difficult year at her school:

One year, it became clear that gossip and side-conversations were getting the best of communication skills from staff to the school board to the parents. At our request, our administration hired an outside mediator to help the staff work through some serious differences and unite us professionally. The staff made a commitment to read a book jointly and discuss it during (some) staff meetings. From the book *Difficult Conversations: How to Discuss What Matters Most*, we shared, practiced, and began to expect direct, respectful communication from colleagues (Stone, Patton, Heen, & Fisher, 2000). It also gave us tools for communication with our larger school community.

Here is a school that recognized it had a problem with its climate and worked collaboratively to fix it. If they hadn't, how many teachers might have been lost? A supportive community of the school staff can help teachers work through any difficulty: challenging parents, poor leadership, or powerful cliques.

HOPE ON THE HORIZON: TEAMING UP WITH TEACHERS

With all the experience teachers have—observing behaviors, learning, and applying teaching techniques daily—as well as their wider view on the reality of schools, they are in a good position to know what works or would work in public education. A report by the Institute for Educational Leadership (2001) pays tribute to teacher contributions:

> Teachers offer something beyond expertise. But at a time when nearly all of public education is in the grip of the rush to politically mandated tests, standards, and account-ability, they may be under heavier pressure than they have ever known. The special qualities that the excellent ones possess—knowledge of children and subject matter, empa-thy, dedication, technique, sensitivity to communities and families, readiness to help, team spirit, ability to communi-cate, and many more—should be in even greater demand than ever. (p. 10)

By teaming up with teachers, school boards can grasp a valuable opportunity. School boards and teachers can collaborate to benefit everyone in the school community, while empowering teachers to know that they are part of school and districtwide leadership.

ADDITIONAL RESOURCES

Print Resources

Alsbury, T. (2008). *The future of school board governance: Relevancy and rev-elation.* Lanham, MD: Rowman & Littlefield.

Eadie, D. (2004). *Five habits of high-impact school boards.* Landham, MD: Scarecrow Education.

Internet Resources

School Advisory Councils in Florida

Florida Department of Education. (n.d.). *School advisory councils: Basic information.* Available from www.flbsi.org/pdf/schad visorycouncil.pdf

Five Characteristics of Effective School Boards

Griffin, A., & Ward, C. D. (2006). *Five characteristics of an effective school board: A multifaceted role, defined.* Available from www.edutopia.org/five-characteristics-effective-school-board

Trained School Boards Save Money

Michigan Association of School Boards. (n.d.). *The importance of school board training.* Available from www.masb.org/Resources Links/TheImportanceofSchoolBoardTraining/tabid/209/Defa ult.aspx

States That Require School Board Training

Petronis, J., Hall, R., & Pierson, M. (1996). *Mandatory school board training: An idea whose time has come?* Available from www.eric.ed.gov/ERICWebPortal/custom/portlets/recordDe tails/detailmini.jsp?_nfpb=true&_&ERICExtSearch_Search Value_0=ED400625&ERICExtSearch_SearchType_0=no& accno=ED400625

Training Your Board to Lead

McAdams, D. R. (2003, November). Training your board to lead. *School Administrator.* Available from www.aasa.org/School AdministratorArticle.aspx?id=8968&terms=training+your+bo ard+to+lead

How to Handle a Bullying Fellow School Board Member

Caruso, N. D. (2006, December). Bullies in the boardroom. *School Administrator.* Available from www.aasa.org/School AdministratorArticle.aspx?id=7386&terms=school+AND+ board+AND+bullying

Afterword:
Final Thoughts

WHY TEACHERS TEACH

Throughout this book there are sections devoted to the many reasons teachers teach despite the ever-growing challenges: a love of children and of knowledge, a deep belief in the democratic ideal of an informed citizenship, the desire to provide equal opportunity to all our children, among others. To be sure, there are less noble reasons as well: a consistent paycheck, the schedule, or the benefits. However, the great majority of teachers look beyond these and also beyond the many challenges discussed in this book. They tend to be idealists. They strive to constantly improve their teaching, public education, and the lives of their students. It is our responsibility as citizens, educational leaders, parents, and politicians to support them in doing so.

None of the problems voiced by teachers and explored in this book will be solved overnight. But many of them can be solved over time, or at least improved, through careful, focused attention. Taking the time to address these issues would work to lessen the tide of teacher attrition and to sustain teachers throughout their careers. As noted in educational research, teachers who are paid more, are valued decision makers and leaders in their schools, have comfortable working conditions, are supported by the administration, and are part of a comprehensive mentoring program as new teachers, are much more likely to continue teaching (National Commission on Teaching and America's Future, 2007). These are solvable problems. It's time for everyone to work together to bring about steady, systematic change in our nation's schools.

TO EDUCATIONAL LEADERS, POLICY MAKERS, AND POLITICIANS

I hope that educational leaders and lawmakers reading this book will gain empathy and understanding of the problems facing teachers today, and that they will take away some ideas for how to make real and meaningful changes to support teachers and students. Here are some final suggestions:

- If every critical parent, politician, and educational leader could substitute in a classroom for at least one day, preferably a few, then they would gain a real sense of what it takes to be a teacher today. Many talk critically of teachers and education without stepping one foot into the shoes of a teacher. Volunteering in your child's classroom is a great way to gain some understanding, but you don't get the whole picture because someone else is fully in charge. Jonathan Kozol, and many other educational writers, commented about how effective and informative this might be in increasing the respect given to teachers and, also, in elevating the dialogue about education to a place of initial empathy and understanding (Kozol, 2007a).

- Seek out teacher feedback on all new educational policies, from the local level to the national level. Teachers bring years of educational experience and an understanding of the current educational climate and challenges. Their input is crucial to making any real and lasting changes. Advisory committees made of teachers can review new policies and provide valuable feedback and perspective. Teachers have lots to say about how the No Child Left Behind legislation has played out in schools and should be instrumental in its revision.

- If school boards remain instrumental to the way we govern our schools, teacher advisory councils could provide assistance, teacher voice, experience, and perspective to assist them in their hard work. To make this motivating and manageable for teachers, school boards and administrators could provide release time or per diem pay. At the very least, procedures for soliciting frequent teacher feedback in school leadership should be developed and utilized.

- Elevate the dialogue about public education by infusing your comments, thoughts, and ideas about education with respect and value for the hard work that teachers are doing in America. As you may have noticed from this book and several others like it, teaching is no easy task. Before making broad and sweeping pronouncements about education, think how your comments will forward the goals of educating children and supporting teachers.

TO TEACHERS

Every day, you are engaged in the hard and beautiful work of educating our nation's children. Here are some final thoughts for you, fellow educators, as you reflect on your profession:

- For many years as a young, new teacher, I was simply working hard, learning the ropes, and trying to do the best I could with my students. I didn't question my school's practices, the comments of my administrators, or the actions of our superintendent or school board. I simply did my job without thinking about the bigger picture. Through the experience of writing this book, I finally learned what Jonathan Kozol (2007a) has been asking of teachers. In *Letters to a Young Teacher,* he wrote:

> When they begin to teach, they come into their classrooms with a sense of affirmation of the goodness and the fullness of existence, with a sense of satisfaction in discovering the unexpected in their students, and with a longing to surprise the world, their kids, even themselves, with their capacity to leave each place they've been (a school, a classroom, a community of learning) a better and more joyful place than when they entered it.
>
> These are the kinds of glowing souls who tend to win the love of children almost without effort. But those who are the recipients of children's love take on responsibilities they sometimes can't anticipate. One of those responsibilities, I think, is the willingness to do away with any semblance of "professional decorum" when such a moment may be called for, and instead to act, no matter what their shyness or their modest self-effacement, as outspoken warriors for justice. . . .

A battle is beginning for the soul of education, and they must be its ultimate defenders. (p. 207–208)

• In my 10 years of teaching, I have learned to speak up for the rights and minds of children in public education, and for the profession of teaching. We need to say what we see and experience, every day in America's schools, and what we know to be true about teaching, education, and our students. Whether it is at a staff meeting, a district committee, a state board of education conference, or a national setting: find your voice.

• It is easy to get lost in the overwhelming minutiae of teaching every day. It is hard to see the forest for the trees and even harder to remember our values, our deepest beliefs. But if we are to continue, to sustain ourselves in this challenging career, we must not only fight for the "soul of education" by advocating for students, best practices, and respect for teachers; we must also nourish our own souls. We've got to remind ourselves why we began teaching in the first place. Who were we? What did we believe? And how can we tap into that for energy, for strength and stamina? One way is simply to write down our core beliefs about education—the ones that motivated us to begin teaching. Then look at how we can live out those beliefs in the classroom or even just make small beginnings. We'll have to look back on this list several times, during standardized testing season, for example. But it will be there. And so will our commitment to it.

It is my deepest hope that teachers who are reading this book will find solace, empathy, understanding, and most important, empowerment in the words of your fellow teachers and in the suggestions and analyses presented here. Remember your core beliefs about life, learning, and teaching, and then let them guide and refresh you.

If teachers, parents, school boards, administrators, community members, and lawmakers can listen to each other and work on this problem together, we can lessen the tide of teacher attrition, ultimately improving the learning and working environment in schools for everyone.

References

Allegretto, S., Corcoran, S., & Mishel, L. (2008). *The teacher penalty: Teacher pay losing ground.* Available from http://epi.3cdn.net/05447667bb274f359e_zam6br3st.pdf

Andrea. (2008, January 2). Re: Teacher burnout? Blame the parents [Msg 7]. Message posted to http://well.blogs.nytimes.com/2008/01/02/teacher-burnout-blame-the-parents

Anonymous. (2008, May 28). Re: Readers' Survey 2008: Amount you spend out of pocket each year on classroom supplies. Message posted to www.edutopia.org/amount-spend-classroom-supplies-2008

Avalon. (2007, December 29). Re: The role of building conditions in school safety [Msg 3]. The Baltimore Sun. Message posted to http://weblogs.baltimoresun.com/news/education/blog/2007/12/the_role_of_building_condition.html

Barrientos, P. (2008, January 2). Re: Teacher burnout? Blame the parents [Msg 19]. Message posted to http://well.blogs.nytimes.com/2008/01/02/teacher-burnout-blame-the-parents

Barth, P. (2008). *Time out: Is recess in jeopardy?* Available from www.centerforpubliceducation.org/site/apps/nlnet/content3.aspx?c=lvIXIiNOJwE&b=5117375&ct=6857723

Barth, R. (2004). *Learning by heart.* San Francisco, CA: Jossey-Bass.

Believe in Yourself - Sherman Dalton [Video file]. (2009, October 17). Available from http://www.youtube.com/watch?v=hsmAw9bJUGg

Borman, G. D., & Dowling, N. M. (2008). Teacher attrition: A meta-analytic and narrative review of the research. *Review of Educational Research, 78*, 367–409.

Brodeur, N. (2008, February 12). Quick fix? Not in our schools. *Seattle Times.* Available from http://seattletimes.nwsource.com/html/nicolebrodeur/2004177633_brodeur12m.html

Brown, D. (2007, May 7). I don't care if you pee on yourself: The test comes first. *Huffington Post.* Available from www.huffingtonpost.com/dan-brown/i-dont-care-if-you-pee-o_b_47874.html

Caspe, M., Lopez, M., & Wolos, C. (2007, Winter). *Family involvement in elementary school children's education.* Available from www.hfrp.org/publications-resources/browse-our-publications/family-involvement-in-elementary-school-children-s-education

Catherine. (2008, January 2). Re: Teacher burnout? Blame the parents [Msg 21]. Message posted to http://well.blogs.nytimes.com/2008/01/02/teacher-burnout-blame-the-parents

Codell, E. (2001). *Educating Esmé: Diary of a teacher's first year.* Chapel Hill, NC: Algonquin Books.

Cox, V. (2004). Guns and roses. In C. Sell (Ed.), *A cup of comfort for teachers* (p. 10). Avon, MA: Adams Media.

Curtis, D. (2000, October 1). Teachers appreciate the value of adequate preparation time. *Edutopia.* Available from www.edutopia.org/treating-teachers-professionals

Curtis, D. (2002, August 1). The freshman principal: Recruiting and retaining effective principals. *Edutopia.* Available from http://www.edutopia.org/freshman-principal

Davis, M. (2007). *Violence against teachers.* Available from http://blogs.edweek.org/edweek/publications/archives/2007/06/violence_agains.html

Delisio, E. (2007, October 23). Mentoring new administrators to success. *Education World.* Available from www.educationworld.com/a_admin/admin/admin465.shtml

Dewey, J. (1933). *How we think.* Boston: D. C. Heath & Co.

Dillon, S. (2006, March 26). Schools cut back subjects to push reading and math. *New York Times.* Available from www.nytimes.com/2006/03/26/education/26child.html?pagewanted=1&_r1

Dr. Bernard. (2008, December 11). Re: Design your own professional development. Message posted to www.edweek.org/forums/?plck ForumPage=ForumDiscussion&plckDiscussionId=Cat%3a047dba4 3-3f1d-45c3-831f-9125f292c0a4Forum%3a349ef86d-a56b-4951-99de-c1838dca95ecDiscussion%3a198e0d48-f25e-4bb5-bd8f-0db4f77c5422&plckCategoryCurrentPage=0

DuFour, R., & Eaker, R. (1998). *Professional learning communities at work.* Bloomington, IN: National Education Service.

Environmental Protection Agency. (2007). *Why do IAQ Tools for Schools? Tools for Schools works!* Available from www.ct.gov/dph/lib/dph/environmental_health/eoha/pdf/TfS_success_stories_fact_sheet.pdf

Environmental Protection Agency. (2010). *IAQ Tools for Schools program.* Available from www.epa.gov/iaq/schools

Flannery, M. E. (2007, November). Why money matters. *NEA Today.* Available from http://www.nea.org/home/14435.htm

Flood, J., & Anders, P. (2005). *Literacy development of students in urban schools.* Newark, DE: International Reading Association.

Florida State University. (2009, January 15). Education professor dispels myths about gifted children. *Science Daily*. Available from http://sciencedaily.com/releases/2009/01/090113123714.htm

George Lucas Educational Foundation. (2008). *Readers' Survey 2008: Amount you spend out of pocket each year on classroom supplies.* Retrieved September 8, 2008, from www.edutopia.org/amount-spend-classroom-supplies-2008

Gomby, D., & Hsieh, K. (n.d.). *Early childhood: Parents and families.* Available from www.abagmd.org/usr_doc/Early_Childhood_-_Parents_and_Families.pdf

Green Schools Initiative. (n.d.). *Executive summary.* Available from http://greenschools.net/article.php?id=124

Guarino, C., Santibanez, L., Daley, G., & Brewer, D. (2004). *A review of the research literature on teacher recruitment and retention.* Available from www.rand.org/pubs/technical_reports/2005/RAND_TR164.sum.pdf

Hinckley, S. (2008, October 30). VPIRG gives state F for Act 125. *Times Argus*. Available from www.timesargus.com/apps/pbcs.dll/article?AID=2008810300368

Institute for Educational Leadership. (2001). *Leadership for student learning: Redefining the teacher as leader.* Available from www.iel.org/programs/21st/reports/teachlearn.pdf

Jeynes, W. (2005). *Parental involvement and student achievement: A meta-analysis.* Available from www.hfrp.org/publications-resources/browse-our-publications/parental-involvement-and-student-achievement-a-meta-analysis

Johnson, S., & Project on the Next Generation of Teachers. (2006, Summer). And why new teachers stay. *American Educator*. Available from http://archive.aft.org/pubs-reports/american_educator/issues/summer06/Teacher.pdf

Kohn, A. (2000, September 27). Standardized testing and its victims. *Education Week*. Available from www.alfiekohn.org/teaching/edweek/staiv.htm

Kopkowski, C. (2008, April). Why they leave. *NEA Today*. Available from www.nea.org/home/12630.htm

Kozol, J. (2007a). *Letters to a young teacher.* New York: Crown Publishers.

Kozol, J. (2007b, September 10). Why I am fasting: An explanation to my friends. *Huffington Post*. Available from www.huffingtonpost.com/jonathan-kozol/why-i-am-fasting-an-expl_b_63622.html

Kumar, D. (2000). *Opportunities for teachers as policy makers.* Available from www.teachnet.org/tnli/resources/kumar.htm

Massachusetts Breastfeeding Coalition. (2008). *For employers.* Available from http://massbfc.org/workplace/#employers

Meier, D., Kohn, A., Darling-Hammond, L., Sizer, T., & Wood, G. (2004). *Many children left behind.* Boston: Beacon Press.

Ms. Pickle. (2006, August 24). Re: 30 minute duty free lunch. Message posted to http://teachers.net/states/la/topic486/8.24.06.17.10.30.html

National Center for Education Statistics. (2007). *Public school principals report on their school facilities: Fall 2005* (NCES 2007-007). Available from http://nces.ed.gov/pubsearch/pubsinfo.asp?pubid=2007007

National Center for Education Statistics. (2008). *Fast facts* [Fact sheet]. Available from http://nces.ed.gov/fastfacts/display.asp?id=28

National Commission on Teaching and America's Future. (n.d.). *Figure 8. School conditions are the biggest reasons for teacher dissatisfaction (1994–1995)* [Data file]. Retrieved June 18, 2009, from www.nctaf .org/documents/charts.pdf

National Commission on Teaching and America's Future. (2003). *No dream denied summary report.* Available from www.nctaf.org/documents/ no-dream-denied_summary_report.pdf

National Commission on Teaching and America's Future. (2007). *NCTAF research reports.* Available from http://www.nctaf.org/ resources/research_and_reports/nctaf_research_reports/index.htm

National Education Association. (2008). *Rankings & estimates* 2008–2009: *Table 1. Average salaries of public school teachers, 2007–2008* [Data file]. Available from www.nea.org/home/29402.htm

National Education Association. (2009a). *Myths and facts about educator pay.* Available from www.nea.org/home/12661.htm

National Education Association. (2009b). *Salary map.* Retrieved February 1, 2009, from www.nea.org/home/20620.htm

National Parent Teacher Association (PTA). (n.d.). *10 things schools/teachers wish parents would do* [Fact sheet]. Available from www.pta.org/Documents/10_Things_Schools.pdf

National Public Radio: Fresh Air (Interviewer), Burd, F. (Interviewee), & Cline, E. (Interviewee). (2007, June 26). *Teaching and trouble in the inner city* [Audio file]. Available from www.npr.org/templates/story/ story.php?storyId=11416891&ampsurl=http%3A//wamu.org/ programs/fresh_air/&ampf=module-FA

National School Boards Association. (1999). *Code of ethics for school board members.* Available from www.nsba.org/MainMenu/Governance/ OtherBoardIssuesResourcesandReportsonSchoolGovernance/Codeof EthicsforSchoolBoardMembers.aspx

Nielsen, S. (2009). *What tired teachers say (when parents aren't listening).* Available from www.oregonlive.com/news/oregonian/susan_nielsen/ index.ssf/2009/11/what_tired_oregon_teachers_say/4284/ comments-5.html

Nieto, S. (2005). *Why we teach.* New York: Teachers College Press.

Northeast Foundation for Children. (2010). *Responsive classroom: About responsive classroom.* Available from www.responsiveclassroom.org/ about/aboutrc.html

Orteacher. (2009, November 15). Re: What tired Oregon teachers say (when parents aren't listening) [Msg 2]. Message posted at www .oregonlive.com/news/oregonian/susan_nielsen/index.ssf/2009/ 11/what_tired_oregon_teachers_say/4284/comments-5.html

Payscale. (2009, May). *Median salary by years experience: All K through 12 teachers (United States)* [Data file]. Available from www.pay scale.com/research/US/All_K12_Teachers/Salary/by_Years_ Experience

Pope, T. (2008). *Teacher burnout? Blame the parents.* Available from http:// well.blogs.nytimes.com/2008/01/02/teacher-burnout-blame-the- parents

Portner, H. (2008, June 1). Committees: Make them more productive. *Teachers Net Gazette.* Available from http://teachers.net/gazette/JUN08/ portner

Rho. (2008, August 6). Re: Readers' Survey 2008: Amount you spend out of pocket each year on classroom supplies. Message posted to www.edutopia.org/amount-spend-classroom-supplies-2008

Robora, A. (2008, December 3). Re: Design your own professional development. Message posted to www.edweek.org/forums/?plckForum Page=ForumDiscussion&plckDiscussionId=Cat%3a047dba43- 3f1d-45c3-831f-9125f292c0a4Forum%3a349ef86d-a56b-4951- 99de-c1838dca95ecDiscussion%3a198e0d48-f25e-4bb5-bd8f-0d b4f77c5422&plckCategoryCurrentPage=0

Rumney Memorial School. (2008a). Discipline procedure. In *The Rumney School parent handbook.* Middlesex, VT: Author.

Rumney Memorial School. (2008b). *Meeting norms.* Middlesex, VT: Author.

Sacks, G. (2001). *Why I am no longer a teacher.* Available from http://www .glennsacks.com/why_im_no.htm

Starr, L. (2006, March 24). Professional learning communities. *Education World.* Available from www.education-world.com/a_curr/ virtualwkshp/virtualwkshp005.shtml

Stone, D., Patton, B., Heen, S., & Fisher, R. (2000). *Difficult conversations: How to discuss what matters most.* New York: Penguin.

Teachers First and National Association of School Psychologists. (n.d.). *Student violence: Warning signs.* Available from www.teachersfirst.com/ crisis/warning.htm

Valdez, S. (2006, September 13). *Lesson plans: The veteran and the rookie.* Available from http://lessonplans.blogs.nytimes.com/2006/09/13/ the-veteran-and-the-rookie

Wei, R. C., Darling-Hammond, L., Andree, A., Richardson, N., & Orphanos, S. (2009). *Professional learning in the learning profession: A status report on teacher development in the United States and abroad.* Available from www.srnleads.org/resources/publications/pdf/nsdc_profdev_tech_ report.pdf

Well Teacher. (n.d.). *Example teacher wellness activities.* Retrieved June 26, 2009, from http://wellteacher.pbwiki.com/f/Example+Teacher+ Wellness+Activities.doc

Whitaker, T., Whitaker, B., & Lumpa, D. (2000). *Motivating and inspiring teachers.* Larchmont, NY: Eye on Education.

Winerip, M. (2009, January 30). Still doing the math, but for 100k a year. *New York Times.* Available from www.nytimes.com/2009/02/ 01/fashion/01generationb.html

Index

Administrators:
    committee meetings, 126–127
    disciplinary pressure, 127–129
    disciplinary procedure, 131–132
    educator recommendations,
        130–132
    job pressure, 122–123
    mentoring relationships,
        129–130, 134–135
    parental pressure, 123–124
    personal days, 125–126
    resources, 135–136
    scenario, 121–122
    testing pressure, 124–125
    time pressure, 125–129
    veteran teachers perspectives, 133
African American students, 13
Andree, A., 52

Barth, R., 44
Bathroom breaks, 27, 31
Behavioral issues:
    administrative discipline, 127–129
    disciplinary procedure, 131–132
    parental involvement,
        101–103, 111
    See also Violent behavior
Borman, G. D., 56, 129
Breastfeeding mothers, 31–32
Building conditions. *See*
    Environmental health; Working
    conditions
Bureaucracy:
    closed budgets, 64–65
    committees, 62–64

educator recommendations,
    69–71
field trips, 59–62, 69
policy, 67–69, 70–71
purchase orders, 64–65, 88
real-life integrated learning, 72–73
resources, 75–76
scenario, 59–60
scheduling time, 65–67, 69–70
teacher dissatisfaction reasons,
    68 (figure)
teaching rationale, 74–75
veteran teachers perspective,
    71–72

Chester School (Connecticut), 36
Closed budgets, 64–65
Codell, E., 63
Collaboration time, 54–55
Collaborative teams:
    local level, 146–147
    school boards, 146–148, 150
    state level, 147–148
Committees:
    administrative meetings, 126–127
    bureaucracy, 62–64
Compensation. *See* Respect and
    compensation; Salary
Connecticut, 35–37
Culture of disrespect, 83–85
Curriculum:
    instructional time per subject,
        8 (figure)
    policy for, 70
    standardized testing effects, 6–9

Darling-Hammond, L., 17, 51
Difficult Conversations (Stone, Patton, Heen, and Fisher), 149
Discipline:
    administrative pressures, 127–129
    disciplinary procedure, 131–132
Dowling, N. M., 56, 129
DuFour, R., 53, 125

Eaker, R., 53, 125
Educating Esmé (Codell), 63
Environmental health:
    educator recommendations, 30, 31
    green schools, 35–37
    impact on instruction,
        25–26 (table)
    permanent buildings, 25 (table)
    portable buildings, 26 (table)
    scenario, 22–23
Environmental Protection Agency
    (EPA), 35–37
Ethics, 143, 144
Expectations:
    collaboration time, 54–55
    educator recommendations, 50–52
    health impact, 47–50, 52–53
    mentoring relationships, 53
    professional development
        limitations, 46–47
    professional development
        recommendations, 52
    professional learning communities,
        53–54
    resources, 57–58
    scenario, 43–44
    teacher wellness activities, 49–50
    teaching rationale, 55–57
    time management, 44–51, 52, 53
    unrealistic expectations, 44
    veteran teachers perspective,
        52–53

Field trips, 59–62, 69
Fisher, R., 149

Grading process, 104–105
Green schools, 35–37

Hamden School (Connecticut), 36
Hartford School (Connecticut), 37
Health and well-being:
    expectations on teachers, 47–50,
        52–53
    teacher wellness activities, 49–50
Heen, S., 149
Helicopter parenting, 103–107

Internal evaluation, 71

Kohn, A., 17
Kozol, J., 16, 155–156

Learning By Heart (Barth), 44, 45
Learning outcomes:
    parental involvement impact,
        99 (figure)
    standardized testing impact,
        9–11
Letters to a Young Teacher (Kozol),
    16, 155–156
Lumpa, D., 31, 51
Lunch breaks, 27–28, 30

Many Children Left Behind (Meier,
    Kohn, Darling-Hammond, Sizer,
    and Wood), 17
Martyr system, 86–88
Meier, D., 17
Mentoring relationships:
    administrators, 129–130,
        134–135
    expectations, 53
Micromanagement, 103–107
Motivating and Inspiring Teachers
    (Whitaker, Whitaker, and
    Lumpa), 31, 51

National School Boards Association
    (NSBA), 143, 144
Nieto, S., 56
No Child Left Behind Act, 5, 10, 13
North Haven School
    (Connecticut), 36

Orphanos, S., 52

Parental involvement:
  administrative pressures, 123–124
  classroom micromanagement,
    103–107
  culture of disrespect, 83–84
  educator recommendations,
    107–113
  grading process, 104–105
  guidelines for, 106
  helicopter parenting, 103–107
  parent-teacher communication,
    100–101, 107–112
  partnering approach, 116–117
  resources, 118–119
  responsive classroom approach,
    112–113
  scenario, 97, 98, 99–100, 103
  school norms, 107–108
  student behavioral issues,
    101–103, 111
  student learning outcomes,
    99 (figure)
  teaching rationale, 117–118
  unrealistic demands and no limits,
    99–101
  veteran teachers perspective,
    113–115
Patton, B., 149
Personal days, 125–126
Policy, 67–69, 70–71
  curriculum planning and
    implementation, 70
  internal evaluation, 71
  school advisory councils, 71
  school-based management, 70–71
  technology, 71
Power dynamics, 140–142
Precautionary principle approach,
    34–35
Professional development:
  limitations of, 46–47
  recommendations for, 52
Professional learning communities,
    53–54
*Professional Learning Communities at
    Work* (DuFour and Eaker),
    53, 125

*Professional Learning in the Learning
    Profession* (Wei, Darling-
    Hammond, Andree, Richardson,
    and Orphanos), 51–52
Purchase orders, 64–65, 88
Purchasing school supplies,
    81–83, 88

Real-life integrated learning, 72–73
Recommendations:
  administrators, 130–132
  bureaucracy, 69–71
  environmental health, 30, 31
  expectations, 50–52
  for policy makers, 154–155
  parental involvement, 107–113
  professional development, 52
  respect and compensation, 88–89
  school boards, 142–145
  standardized testing, 14–15
  to teachers, 155–156
  working conditions, 28–32
Resources:
  administrators, 135–136
  bureaucracy, 75–76
  parental involvement, 118–119
  teacher expectations, 57–58
  working conditions, 37–41
  See also Website resources
Respect and compensation:
  culture of disrespect, 83–85
  decent working wage, 90
  educator recommendations,
    88–89
  making ends meet, 77–81
  martyr system, 86–88
  purchasing school supplies,
    81–83, 88
  raising teacher compensation,
    90–91, 94
  resources, 96
  salary, 78, 79 (figure), 90–91,
    92–93 (figure)
  scenario, 77, 83–84, 90
  teaching rationale, 94–96
  veteran teachers perspective,
    89–90

Responsive classroom approach,
    112–113
Review of Educational Research
    (Borman and Dowling), 56, 129
Richardson, N., 52
Role playing, 111

Salary:
    average salaries per state,
        92–93 (table)
    median salary by years experience,
        79 (figure)
    profession comparisons, 78
    raising teacher compensation,
        90–91, 943
    See also Respect and compensation
Scheduling:
    and bureaucracy, 65–67, 69–70
    bathroom breaks, 27, 31
    lunch breaks, 27–28, 30
    standardized testing, 9–11
    See also Time management
School advisory councils, 71
School-based management, 70–71
School boards:
    code of ethics, 143, 144
    collaborative teams, 146–148, 150
    educator recommendations,
        142–145
    power dynamics, 140–142
    resources, 150–151
    scenario, 137–138
    shared leadership, 138–140
    teaching rationale, 148–150
    veteran teachers perspective,
        145–146
School climate, 6
School conditions. *See* Environmental
    health; Working conditions
School norms, 107–108
School violence, 19, 20–23, 28–29
Shared leadership, 138–140
Sizer, T., 17
Socioeconomic status (SES), 12–13
Standardized testing:
    administrative testing pressures,
        124–125
    curriculum effects, 6–9

curriculum instructional time,
    8 (figure)
educator recommendations,
    14–15
learning outcome effects, 9–11
reevaluation of, 17
resources for, 17–18
scenario, 5
scheduling effects, 9–11
school climate effects, 6
student effects, 11–14
teaching rationale, 16
veteran teachers perspective,
    15–16
Stone, D., 149

Teaching rationale:
    autonomy, 55–56
    challenging and always changing,
        55–57
    community contribution, 117–118
    creativity, 55–56
    helping children learn and grow,
        94–96
    longevity requirements, 153
    making a difference, 74–75
    personal fulfillment, 16
    supportive communities, 148–150
Technology, 71
Time management:
    administrative time pressures,
        125–129
    collaboration time, 44–51, 52, 53
    expectations, 44–51, 52, 53
    personal days, 125–126
    See also Scheduling
Tools for Schools Program, 35–37

Unsafe schools, 22–24,
    25–26 (table), 28

Violent behavior, 19, 20–23, 28–29
    at-risk students, 22

Waterford School (Connecticut), 36
Website resources:
    administrators, 135–136
    bureaucracy, 76

expectations, 57–58
parental involvement, 118–119
respect and compensation, 96
school boards, 151
standardized testing, 18
working conditions, 37–41
Wei, R. C., 51
Whitaker, B., 31, 51
Whitaker, T., 31, 51
Why We Teach (Nieto), 56
Wood, G., 17
Working conditions:
bathroom breaks, 27, 31
breastfeeding mothers, 31–32
building repairs, 24
educator recommendations, 28–32
environmental health, 22–23,
    25–26 (table), 30, 31
green schools, 35–37
lunch breaks, 27–28, 30
permanent buildings, 25 (table)
portable buildings, 26 (table)
precautionary principle approach,
    34–35
resources for, 37–41
scenario, 19, 22–23, 27, 33–34
unsafe schools, 22–24,
    25–26 (table), 28
veteran teachers' perspective,
    33–34
violent behavior, 19, 20–23,
    28–29

CORWIN

A SAGE Company

The Corwin logo—a raven striding across an open book—represents the union of courage and learning. Corwin is committed to improving education for all learners by publishing books and other professional development resources for those serving the field of PreK–12 education. By providing practical, hands-on materials, Corwin continues to carry out the promise of its motto: **"Helping Educators Do Their Work Better."**